# Effective Problem Solving

## A structured approach

Dave Francis

London

First published 1990
by Routledge
11 New Fetter Lane, London EC4P 4EE


© 1990 Dave Francis

Printed and bound in Great Britain by
Biddles Ltd, Guildford and King's Lynn

*British Library Cataloguing in Publication Data*

Francis, Dave
    Effective problem solving.
    1. Management. Problem solving
    I. Title    II. Series
    658.403

ISBN 0-415-05357-9

PO 2188

# *Contents*

# *Preface*

The 1990s represent a period of challenge and change which brings with it the need for managers to have skills and capabilities that will enable them to respond to the demands put upon them. The *Self-development for Managers* series has been created to provide managers with the opportunity to build necessary expertise.

Effective problem solving was recognized as essential to managers for dealing with the situations that arise in a rapidly changing environment. The book clearly identifies these situations, categorizing them as difficulties, puzzles, opportunities and dilemmas.

This book gives the reader a thorough understanding of the steps that must be followed in order to solve problems effectively. Readers have the opportunity to assess their problem-solving skills and are given a range of techniques to help them undertake each of the steps. The project enables managers to apply the tools and techniques to a situation of their choosing.

*Effective Problem Solving* complements other books in the series. Most management issues can be better addressed if the manager uses a proven approach to problem solving.

Dave Francis has worked with managers for over fifteen years in his capacity as an independent consultant. In this time he has developed an excellent approach to problem solving which can be used in a wide range of situations. The approach has been applied in a variety of industries including manufacturing, insurance, the health service and retailing. Hundreds of managers have benefited from this well-developed method of tackling problems. Dave's lucid writing and his wealth of practical experience make him a valuable contributor to the series.

Jane Cranwell-Ward

# *Introduction*

Management is a craft in the medieval sense of the word. Mastery requires a combination of science, art, practical experience, and learning from accomplished masters. As with any craft, there are disciplines to follow and tools to use. This book is about one of the most important disciplines in the craft of management – problem solving.

We all have obstacles to overcome and mountains to climb. Effective management is about resolving difficult issues. But don't despair: the structured approach described in this book will assist you to solve problems logically and effectively.

This book advocates a structured approach to problem solving. Anyone who doubts the value of structure only has to attend aerobics classes twice a week for three months. Simply learn the routines, do what you are told, and the structured exercises (which are the encapsulated wisdom of many contributors) will get you fit.

The structured approach to problem solving described in this book is known by the acronym TOSIDPAR (much more about this later). It is important that I tell you the truth before you start. The methods described are not easy to master. Initially this comprehensive and integrated tool kit of management techniques needs to be followed as a strict discipline. Later the TOSIDPAR approach will become second nature and you will use it with poise and flexibility.

Mastering the TOSIDPAR structured approach to problem solving is like learning to drive a car. On the first driving lesson everything seems to happen at once and the novice is invariably confused and overwhelmed. With practice the basic craft skills of driving are learned but it still requires enormous concentration to drive safely. Gradually driving becomes second nature, and the disciplines become embedded in the person's unconscious repertoire of skills.

The TOSIDPAR structured approach is the hallmark of a professional who favours thoroughness rather than cosmetically attractive, quick solutions. It is vital for all managers to be able to use the full TOSIDPAR approach, just as it is critical for a surgeon to be able to use all surgical instruments.

Managers often raise an important objection: they fear that a structured approach would be so time-consuming that nothing would ever get done! There is an element of truth in this concern. The full approach, using all of the techniques described, is truly laborious. But this is a strength rather than a weakness: TOSIDPAR is a rigorous discipline dedicated to providing truly effective action programmes. However, there are shortcuts explained in Chapter 12 which transform TOSIDPAR from being a specialist methodology into an everyday mangement discipline.

This book is dedicated to promoting the creative use of structure. Its aim is to help you become more effective. A word of caution: it will be beneficial if, and only if, you actually use the TOSIDPAR approach on real issues. The project and exercises are not optional extras but essential elements. You will have to do some work!

This is a practical book, which includes the necessary theory to explain the steps. 'Simple without being simplistic' is the aim. The book's primary audience is managers, supervisors, students of management, teachers, professional workers, trainers, and consultants. But don't let this inhibit you if you are a trapeze artist, dog breeder, or the curator of Egyptian mummies in a museum. Effective problem solvers are made, not born. Skills in solving problems and getting things done are life skills, needed by everyone. In fact, I firmly believe that they should be taught in schools!

This book is often used as the core text in educational or training programmes designed to develop skills in problem solving. If you are about to attend such a course, read the book and undertake the project before you attend. Use the assignments given to you on the course as laboratory experiments to test your understanding of the TOSIDPAR structured approach. Then (sorry about this) read the book again to consolidate your understanding.

If you are not able to attend a course it is perfectly possible to master the techniques yourself. One piece of advice: many people find that it is easier to learn with others. For this reason it is useful to have a support group of kindred spirits who go through a process of development together. Agree to learn from each other's experience and give the others totally honest feedback. A supportive, confronting, and active group is the best environment to help you learn.

The TOSIDPAR structured approach to problem solving becomes even more powerful when it becomes a common set of skills practised by all members of management teams. Organizational sociologists rightly point out that a lone individual intent on change is weakened by constantly fighting against the prevailing culture. It is best if all members of management use a common language; otherwise we have the organizational equivalent of the Tower of Babel.

When a craftsworker goes to a new job, he or she takes along a bag of tools. The effective problem solver needs a range of conceptual or process tools to be used as appropriate. Throughout this book you will find that basic problem-solving tools have been described. You are encouraged to try each tool and adapt it to suit your particular needs.

Don't imagine that it is going to be easy to become more effective in the art and science of getting things done. You are not starting from scratch. Over the years you have met many mysteries, assignments, difficulties, opportunities, puzzles, and dilemmas – and done your best. You, as the police say, already have an MO (modus operandi). Some of your habits will be unconstructive or inefficient. These negative habits need to be detected, understood, and changed.

Although it may appear pretentious, it is true to say that the effective person has followed the ancient admonition, 'know thyself'. You might think that being effective just requires a comprehensive toolkit of relevant techniques. But this is naïve. People have been endlessly trained in all the relevant techniques and it has made little difference to their real-life capability. Why? Something has blocked their use of the skills; perhaps negative attitudes, sloppy thinking, or a lack of assertion. True effectiveness requires much more than a handful of skills or techniques. We will explore these potential blockages to effective problem solving in the first three chapters of the book.

In writing this book I acknowledge the ideas presented here

have come from many sources. The action research programme which provided the framework for this book was begun in 1975 with United Biscuits in England. The greatest debt is owed to the several thousand people who have participated in my training programmes in many countries during the past twenty years. In particular I am grateful to my many friends at Associated British Ports, the Commercial Union Assurance Company, Henley Management College, Hong Kong Telephone, Inmos, Jardine Pacific, Lion Brewery of New Zealand, Plessey, Polygram, Save the Children Fund, Smithkline Beecham, and Thorn EMI.

Finally, writing a book is a big project: at once an assignment and opportunity, and a source of difficulties and dilemmas. I would like to thank Jane Cranwell-Ward for being an excellent supervising editor. She has made the book a better piece of work.

Problem solving is the lifeblood of management. The craft must be learnt in the real world. No matter how much theory you acquire, the only valid tests are those which life throws at you. Practice the stances and skills explained in this book as much as you can. Stand back, review your successes and failures, and challenge yourself. Then celebrate your growing competence.

# 1 *Introducing TOSIDPAR*

Careful research[1] has shown that most managers undertake between fifty and seventy projects at any moment. All managers face the challenge of trying to avoid being overwhelmed by a cascade of demands. Effective managers are compelled to use a flexible structured approach to get things done.

A structured approach is a universal toolkit. For many generations, novice doctors, army officers, engineers, and police inspectors have found that their basic training encourages them to adopt a structured methodology in almost every situation. A structured approach reduces individual bias, ensures rigour, and provides an essential helpmate in times of difficulty.

Structured processes are especially needed by those who run organizations. In the last fifty years, management has been the fastest growing profession. Today, there are more people employed as managers and supervisors than any other professional group. Every manager needs a multipurpose structured approach that is capable of resolving such disparate issues as whether to discipline an air stewardess who is (almost certainly) selling illicit champagne to determining what will be the likely developments in semiconductor technology over the next five years.

The approach described throughout the remainder of this book is one way[2] for developing the competencies of managers – and others who are interested in the art and science of getting things done. The structured approach is known by the acronym TOSIDPAR – not an elegant term but precise in its meaning. The structured approach has eight separate steps, each of which requires specialized skills and techniques. It is not a rigid approach; capable problem solvers use TOSIDPAR flexibly.

Capable problem solvers see each problem as a separate project. Each has to be started afresh. Using old recipes for problem solving prematurely closes the mind. The eight steps of TOSIDPAR are explained at length later in the book (there is a chapter on each) but here is a brief introduction:

## STEP ONE: TUNING IN – To get you started

The first step in problem solving is to 'tune in'. This means developing a clear overall appreciation (by all involved) of the nature of the presenting issue and the kind of challenges being undertaken. If a team is needed, the members chosen must have the necessary technical skills and energy – and they must be capable of relating well with each other. Roles and responsibilities are provisionally allocated. Time constraints and resource limitations are assessed. Tuning in enables the capable problem solver to answer the questions: What kind of task is this? And what challenges does it present?

## STEP TWO: OBJECTIVE SETTING – To clarify what you want

The second step is objective setting: this requires becoming entirely clear about what end results are wanted. It is not easy. People prefer to get into action rather than devote effort to clarifying objectives. Objectives need to be as specific as possible, exciting, and understood by all concerned. Capable problem solvers ensure that objectives are lucid and provide a necessary focus.

## STEP THREE: SUCCESS MEASURES – To establish yardsticks

The third step involves defining 'success'. Capable managers emphasize that measurement is perhaps the most important activity undertaken. Often considerable effort needs to be expended to determine the appropriate success criteria (a definition of success) and success measures (how progress will be monitored).

## STEP FOUR: INFORMATION COLLECTION – To gather and structure data

The fourth step involves the collection and understanding of new facts, opinions, feelings, ideas, and attitudes about the project. Information is drawn from experience and knowledge, external sources, and research. The skills involved include creative thinking, identifying relevant data, collecting valid data, structuring data to make sense, identifying gaps in information, and meeting them. A blend of free-flowing creativity and highly disciplined analysis is required. The information step is complete when options for action are clearly laid out.

## STEP FIVE: DECISION MAKING – To make the best possible choice about what to do

The fifth step is concerned with assessing the available options and making the best decision about what to do. This involves organizing and displaying options so that they are totally clear and then stating unambiguously what criteria will be used to assess each option. Risks need to be explicit and measured. The decision-making step is complete when a clear choice has been made about what will be done.

## STEP SIX: PLANNING – To control and co-ordinate resources to get things done

The sixth step provides a detailed programme to effect decisions. Plans are mechanisms to determine who does what, where, when, and how. Plans also consider how to cope with potential snags – foreseen or unforeseen. The planning step is complete when issues concerning the following seven issues are resolved: co-ordination, control, communication, specifications, priorities, resource management, and sequencing.

## STEP SEVEN: ACTION – To implement plans creatively

The seventh step ensures that plans are implemented and the necessary tasks undertaken. If the previous steps have been well tackled there is a good chance of success – but adaptability is necessary. It is necessary to recycle the TOSIDPAR process quickly if things go awry.

## STEP EIGHT: REVIEW TO IMPROVE – To learn from the experience

The eighth step provides a structured opportunity to learn from the experience. The purpose is twofold: first, to check if the task was successful – whether the specific objectives were met; and second, to improve methods in the future. We learn from analysing successes and identifying the causes of failure. Feedback is crucial for improvement.

It is helpful to see the TOSIDPAR approach in diagram format (see figure opposite). This helps us visualize how each step evolves from the previous step and logically leads to the next. Each of the eight steps of TOSIDPAR has several distinct stages and a distinct set of skills – a 'technology' of its own. The capable problem solver can use the TOSIDPAR approach with great flexibility based on disciplined training.

There are no shortcuts to learning. Disciplines must be acquired before they can be abandoned. Managers are advised to master all the steps of TOSIDPAR before they allow themselves to extemporize (more about this in Chapter 12).

**TOSIDPAR: A structure for problem solving**

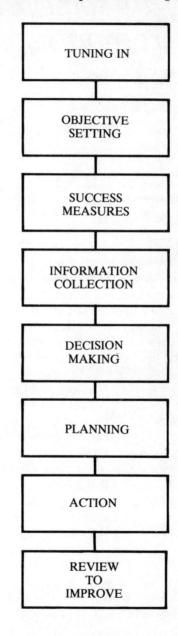

# 2 Why are some problem solvers more capable than others?

In the last chapter we learned that capable problem solvers are master craftsmen in using the TOSIDPAR structured approach to get things done. Are there not other essential attributes which are needed?

Two questions are important: Do capable problem solvers behave differently from the rest of us? If so, how does their behaviour differ? Answer these questions with precision and we have a template to evaluate our own problem-solving capability.

The best way to define the characteristics of a capable problem solver is to see what competencies they possess. A competency is the bundle of underlying characteristics that enables individuals to operate at a superior level. There are four essential attributes:

- **Strong motivation** — Capable problem solvers want to defeat difficulties with all their energy
- **Positive traits** — Capable problem solvers have the personal characteristics that enable them to succeed
- **Powerful self-image** — Capable problem solvers see themselves as powerful people but are realistic about their limitations
- **Developed skills** — Capable problem solvers have learned abilities that enable them to use relevant skills and techniques

## STRONG MOTIVATION

Capable problem solvers want to defeat difficulties with all their energy. They adopt a positive set of attitudes towards adversity.

6

For them it's war, a war they intend to win. Difficulties are welcomed because they give the problem solver a chance to overcome barriers, demonstrate superior prowess, and complete tasks that other people find difficult or arduous.

The capable problem solver is energized, not weakened, by problems and difficulties. Winning is a drug. He or she has a view of the world which sees adversity as inevitable but temporary. Their belief is that a better future can and must be created. When a quandary comes along, the capable problem solver senses inner excitement or a surge of strength. Sometimes you can see the signs expressed non-verbally: the chin juts forward and the lip curls as if the person were saying, 'Damn it, this will not beat me!'

Capable problem solvers redouble commitment when things go wrong. They rarely feel trounced by mysteries or difficulties. This point is well made when we look at the work undertaken by Thomas Edison to perfect the incandescent lightbulb. He had performed over 9,000 experiments when one of his associates asked him, 'Why do you persist with this folly? You have failed more than nine thousand times.' Edison replied, 'I haven't even failed once; nine thousand times I have learnt what doesn't work.'

## POSITIVE TRAITS

The personal characteristics of capable problem solvers enable them to succeed. Such a person has an interesting psychological make-up. He or she stands back emotionally from a problem and makes an objective assessment. This does not mean the capable problem solver is uncommitted; in fact, the opposite is the case. Truly effective problem solvers are passionately interested in anything that blocks their progress and throw themselves wholeheartedly into finding effective solutions.

The psychological traits of objectivity and commitment are crucial, but they are not enough. Equally important is a willingness to accept help from others. The capable problem solver often works with other people to get things done.

Now comes a delicate issue: capable problem solvers are intelligent. Don't be nervous; they are not all super-brains, just sufficiently bright to understand the issues. Of course, some difficult problems (for example, why do some aircraft suffer from metal fatigue earlier than others?) require a great deal of scientific know-how and intellectual sharpness. Fortunately, difficult issues can be solved by most managers if they use a comprehensive structured approach, but capable problem solvers understand when a situation is too difficult.

The final necessary psychological trait has an old-fashioned ring to it. Capable problem solvers have persistence or, as Baden-Powell called it, 'stickability'. They do not easily give up. When the rest of us are daunted, the capable problem solver feels disappointment but channels that energy into a renewed attack, Perhaps the best examples come from police work: in one murder case the police interviewed 154,000 people before finding a lead. Only their persistence and unwillingness to be defeated resulted in a conviction.

## POWERFUL SELF-IMAGE

Capable problem solvers see themselves as powerful people but are realistic about their limitations. They have a great deal of self-confidence and feel in charge of the situations that arise. They avoid the pervasive cynicism that undermines so many people's potency. They adopt the motto: 'I am able to get this done.'

Self-confidence, like any virtue, can be excessive, especially if it is unrealistic. In the English seaside resort of Brighton there is a Victorian pier that has fallen into disrepair. The company that owned it realized that millions were needed to return the pier to its previous splendour, and that there was little likelihood of an adequate return on the investment. Thus the pier was put up for sale for one penny with the buyer responsible for refurbishment. There was consternation in the office on the day following the announcement of the sale as a small boy, clutching a penny, came in to buy the pier. He had ample self-confidence but it was built on unrealistic foundations.

The capable problem solver feels able, even when he or she does not know what to do. Possessing this psychological capacity, known as the 'tolerance of ambiguity', is crucial. Invariably, overcoming obstacles requires entering a period of uncertainty. This does not weaken the capable problem solver, who simply sees uncertainty as a companion on the journey towards solving a problem.

# DEVELOPED SKILLS

Capable problem solvers can use all of the techniques of TOSIDPAR. Often these are straightforward, although for complex technical projects advanced tools are necessary.

Imagine a situation which must occur many times a day in companies around the world. A group of managers are brought together to decide what to do in the light of a threatening new product which is to be launched by a competitor. The group have to formulate a defensive competitive strategy.

The manager who convened the meeting has exercised a number of skills before all arrive. Participants have been selected, briefed, and given preliminary work to do. The meeting room has been prepared with a wide range of visual aids. Interruptions have been prevented. There is a secretary on hand to take notes. The competitor's new product has been purchased, broken down, and assessed. Several individuals have prepared presentations that describe the likely threat. An agenda has been circulated.

Once the meeting starts new skills are required, especially from the person who is chairing the meeting. Everyone must know the relevant facts and feel the importance of the competitor's threat. The objectives of the meeting must be in the forefront of everyone's mind. All members must have an opportunity to contribute, but not to dominate the meeting. Options for action need to be clarified and tasks assigned. Creativity is encouraged but the meeting cannot be allowed to end on a note of divergent fancy; a coherent action plan must emerge which commits everyone to the outcome.

These are just a few of the many skills that need to be acquired: the problem solver's overall ability is the result of having all the necessary skills and being able to use them flexibly according to the needs of the situation.

# THE CAPABLE PROBLEM SOLVER

We have begun to explore the competencies needed for successful problem solving. In fact, there are forty distinct attributes that capable problem solvers demonstrate. It is now time for you to do some work! Complete the 'capability audit' below in relation to your own current capabilities. Try to be honest and objective – neither excessively self-critical nor over-confident. Put a tick in one of the three columns as appropriate. When you have completed all the items go back over the audit and circle the three items that you feel it would be most helpful to work on over the next few months. Then complete the exercise as suggested at the end.

Just before you begin, you might like to take several photocopies of the 'capability audit' (permitted by copyright restrictions for your own personal use only), give one to your boss, friends, co-workers, and subordinates, and ask them to fill it in about you. This will provide you with more objective data and the chance to obtain interesting feedback on your problem-solving prowess.

## Capability audit

| Attributes | OK | Need to do more | Need to do better |
|---|---|---|---|
| 1  Wanting to defeat problems | | | |
| 2  Welcoming problems as opportunities | | | |
| 3  Being energized, not weakened, by problems | | | |
| 4  Seeing difficulties as temporary | | | |
| 5  Believing that a better future can be created | | | |
| 6  Redoubling effort when things go wrong | | | |
| 7  Rarely being beaten by problems | | | |
| 8  Being able to stand back emotionally from problems | | | |
| 9  Being passionately interested in finding the solution to problems | | | |
| 10  Working with others to solve problems | | | |
| 11  Understanding own limits of intelligence | | | |
| 12  Being persistent when things go wrong | | | |
| 13  Having realistic self-confidence | | | |
| 14  Not being cynical | | | |

| Attributes | OK | Need to do more | Need to do better |
|---|---|---|---|
| 15 Feeling capable despite uncertainty | | | |
| 16 Adopting a logical and systematic approach to problem solving | | | |
| 17 Not being rigid when analysing problems | | | |
| 18 Always being aware of the impediments to effective problem solving | | | |
| 19 Seeing problems as projects to be undertaken | | | |
| 20 Not using old recipes for new problems | | | |
| 21 Identifying the type of challenges being faced | | | |
| 22 Choosing the best team to tackle a problem | | | |
| 23 Understanding time and resource constraints | | | |
| 24 Specifying objectives to be achieved | | | |
| 25 Establishing systems to measure success | | | |
| 26 Collecting information in a systematic manner | | | |
| 27 Creatively generating new information | | | |
| 28 Structuring information so that it makes sense | | | |
| 29 Encouraging the expression of feelings and intuition | | | |
| 30 Developing clear options for action | | | |
| 31 Developing criteria to evaluate options for action | | | |
| 32 Establishing the difference between essential and desirable criteria in decision making | | | |

| Attributes | OK | Need to do more | Need to do better |
|---|---|---|---|
| 33  Breaking tasks down into 'bite-sized' chunks | | | |
| 34  Scheduling tasks in sequence | | | |
| 35  Specifying standards to be achieved | | | |
| 36  Developing effective co-ordinating mechanisms | | | |
| 37  Acting with vigour and commitment | | | |
| 38  Taking time to review to improve | | | |
| 39  Learning from both successes and failures | | | |
| 40  Giving feedback to help all involved to improve their contribution in the future | | | |

## CAPABILITY AUDIT REVIEW

Consider the forty items listed above and identify three that you feel it is most important for you to work on over the next few months. Also consider feedback that you have received from others. Write the items (not just the numbers) in the spaces provided and, in discussion with at least one other person, brainstorm practical ways in which you can develop your problem-solving capability in the months to come. Seek clear actions that you can take within your present situation.

| Selected three items | Ideas on how to improve |
|---|---|
| 1 | |
| 2 | |
| 3 | |

# 3 When is a problem not a problem?

Investigating why some people suddenly discover flies in their tap water, producing a report for the top management committee, informing a highly strung employee that his personal hygiene is inadequate, wondering how to take a new soap powder to market, finding a lost city of the Incas, or deciding whether to give up a career as a personnel director to become a teacher – these are usually all called 'problems'. In fact, these six are different. The first is a mystery, the next an assignment, the third a difficulty, the forth an opportunity, the fifth a puzzle, and the last a dilemma.

It is important to distinguish between mysteries, assignments, difficulties, opportunities, puzzles, and dilemmas because each requires a special approach, especially in the first four analytical steps of the structured TOSIDPAR approach. Ordinary language, which calls everything difficult 'a problem', is too unrefined for our purposes.

## MYSTERIES

A mystery is 'an unexplained deviation from what is expected'. This definition emphasizes the word 'unexplained'. If something is happening that is different from our expectations and we don't know the reason, then we have a mystery. When the astronauts of Apollo 13 experienced an almost catastrophic explosion in their spacecraft on the way to the moon, they called mission control and said that they had a malfunction that they could not explain: a mystery. Immediately the technical teams in Houston gathered into problem-solving teams to explore the mystery. Their analytical skills and creative brilliance brought the astronauts home.

The most important aspect of a mystery is that we do not know the cause. Accordingly, all our effort must be directed to finding out why we have 'an unexplained deviation from what is expected'. Sometimes causes are easy to discover, but often they are not. I visited a company making electronic components to discuss a mystery in the production process for manufacturing state-of-the-art printed circuit boards. Too many scrap products were being produced and no one knew why. The manager said, 'It's a weird situation. We just don't know what the hell is happening. All the usual remedies have been tried.' But the mystery persisted. Every ounce of managerial brainpower had been dedicated to finding the causes but they still did not know what was going wrong. Perhaps twenty chemicals were mixed in a vat and kept at a designated temperature. One or more of the chemicals was not doing its job, but which one and why? Was it the same chemical every time? Did all the printed circuit boards suffer from exactly the same defect? The managers in this factory faced a genuine mystery. What happened? In the end, after weeks of analysis, it emerged that an operator had been disciplined some months earlier for drinking whisky on the job and was wreaking vengeance by deliberately allowing static electricity to contaminate some of the products.

Unless there are measurable standards of what should happen, you are not able to detect mysteries. For example, a salesman is expected to obtain at least 150 new orders each month. For years this has been regularly achieved; then the pattern changes. The recent numbers of monthly sales achieved are 164, 155, 151, 147, 144, 145, 141. The sales manager has a mystery: she does not know why the deviation has occurred. Without measurable standards, all mysteries remain in the background.

Not all mysteries are bad. Sometimes something goes right but we don't know the reasons why. A worldwide music company found that their Scandinavian region produced consistently better results than the other areas. No one really knew the reasons: it was an unexplained deviation from what was expected. Sensibly, the company undertook an investigation and found that the Scandinavian marketing department had developed creative concepts that could be transferred to the other regions. The mystery was solved and the whole company benefited.

# ASSIGNMENTS

It often happens that we are given a task to do. This is an assignment: a situation in which you are not the originator of the requirement. The boss will say one day, 'I want you to prepare a report on the feasibility of towing icebergs from the Antarctic to Saudi Arabia as a source of fresh water.' You are given your goals and, like the woodwind section of the orchestra, you are required to play a part in a larger whole.

Assignments require special techniques because goals have to be communicated downwards. Those undertaking assigned tasks must ensure that they understand the purposes of their work and the parameters that have been set (schedules, resource allocation, success criteria, etc.). Often such task are interdependent with others, and the overall purpose must be well understood.

An assignment is a kind of contract: an agreement between a boss (or client) and the person who is going to carry out the task. A consultant receives an assignment on accepting a project, a doctor gives an assignment when she tells the patient what medicine to take, and a customer delivers an assignment when she tells the hairdresser how she wants her hair to look. In each case it is imperative that the contract is understood, explicit, achievable, and agreed.

# DIFFICULTIES

Some things are difficult to accomplish. Often we know what needs to be done but the execution is demanding, exacting, or intricate. Imagine that you are a tennis player about to play a final at Wimbledon: you are a top world-class tennis player but are aware that there is much at stake. If you play your best for the next three hours your name will be given an honoured place in tennis history books; if you fail, you will be seen by the world as an also-ran. But you feel sick and already sense that you are about to lose. You have a difficulty.

A difficulty occurs for two reasons: either we do not know how to manage the situation or feel that we lack adequate resources. Accordingly, to resolve a difficulty all our effort must be directed to solving the managerial blockage and acquiring the necessary resources.

Often we become accustomed to difficulties and live with them as if they were unchangeable realities. A personal experience makes the point. My mother loved books; she was an avid reader all her life. As she became afflicted with arthritis in her hands, it became hard for her to hold a book. She virtually gave up reading. Once I became aware of her difficulty I visited the Disabled Living Foundation where I found an ingenious holder which held books in exactly the right position for reading. The difficulty had been detected, brought into the foreground, and resolved.

Difficulties can be divided into two categories: subjective and objective. In the case of a subjective difficulty, the impediment or blockage lies within the person. The person has the capability but, for some reason·or other, is unable to accomplish what needs to be done. The Wimbledon tennis player described above has a subjective difficulty.

In the case of an objective difficulty, the impediment or blockage lies outside of the person. Achieving the desired end results is unlikely or impossible. At the age of fourteen I recall trying to build a space rocket with another schoolboy, using tin cans and gunpowder salvaged from fireworks. We survived but the rocket only went a metre off the ground. We lacked everything – talent, know-how, resources, and motivation. Objective difficulties rendered our plan to explore space totally impossible.

Not all objective difficulties are insurmountable. For example, establishing an oil rig in the deserts of western China presents many obstacles: there are few roads, the heat is almost unbearable, water is unavailable, local labourers lack skills, the Chinese administrative system is cumbersome, and so on. Hundreds of difficulties abound; although each can be vanquished, the complexity of the whole task would test the most experienced oil man. The key issues in determining whether an objective difficulty is surmountable are resource availability and planning capability.

From a strategic point of view the capacity to overcome difficulties provides an organization with a layer of competitive advantage. Hence, as we will explore further below, one person's difficulty can become an opportunity for someone else.

# OPPORTUNITIES

Although some days it may not feel true, good things do sometimes happen! A chance to do something differently or better can pop out of the blue. Opportunities can either be created or happen through serendipity and providence.

The most important thing about an opportunity is that it offers a potential benefit. Our efforts should be directed to creating opportunities, detecting them when they occur, and rapidly exploiting the chance to gain advantage.

In the early days of plain paper photocopying, the vital patents were held by the Xerox Corporation which were making a king's ransom out of their monopoly of this superior technology. Although they did not know it, the Canon company in Japan had identified Xerox's apparently unassailable dominance as an opportunity. Xerox specialized in printroom-sized equipment, but virtually ignored the potential market for small copiers. Here was Canon's chance: the company set up a team to find new techniques for plain paper copying that did not infringe Xerox's patents. The rest of the story is apparent to anyone who visits a modern office with Canon copiers; Canon saw an opportunity and transformed it into a highly successful strategy.

There is a delightful, and true, story about an entrepreneur who saw an opportunity. He realized that many people went into tobacconist shops and said 'Box 'er matches, please'. So our entrepreneur produced a brand of matches called 'Boxer Matches'. Tobacconists thought that the customer was after that particular brand and Boxer Matches thrived for many years. That's opportunism!

Not all opportunities occur in fresh pastures. Often opportunities exist because current ways of doing things do not maximize their potential. Until the early 1980s the Toyota Motor company had two major divisions: one concerned with manufacturing and the other with sales. The manufacturing division took only two days to produce a car but the sales division required between thirteen and twenty-four days to process the order. To make matters worse, the costs of running the sales division swallowed up the benefits of a super-efficient manufacturing system. Obviously there was an opportunity and the two divisions were joined in 1982. By 1987 Toyota was taking only eight days to make and deliver a car from first receiving the customer's order.

There are irritating people who pounce on anyone who uses the word 'problem' and say, with great sonorousness, 'I don't have problems: every problem is an opportunity'. As we mentioned above, the observation is partly correct. At first, it seems illogical as opportunities provide advantage and problems are sources of disadvantage. However, solving a problem or overcoming a difficulty can give birth to an opportunity.

This argument can be taken further. Michael Porter has undertaken international research on the sources of national competitive advantage.[1] His conclusions are profound. Only industries that learn to overcome the most intractable difficulties grow into world-class players. The Dutch Flower industry is a case in point. Holland's climate makes it difficult to grow flowers, so the Dutch learned to control every step of the process in well-regulated and economical greenhouses. Their expertise, drawn from their experience in overcoming adversity, provided an opportunity. Today, as you read this, the flower sellers of New York are offering blooms picked yesterday in a Dutch greenhouse, while countries with more natural advantages have failed to exploit them.

Opportunism is more than a set of techniques: it is a positive state of mind. The opportunist is awake to chances, and willing to accept a proportion of failures. In a sense the opportunist is a modern-day hunter, no longer seeking the woolly mammoth but searching for a business coup or lifestyle boon.

## PUZZLES

There are some situations in which we know that a correct answer exists, but we do not know what it is. Such situations are puzzles: only some answers can be right and the rest are wrong. It is as simple as that. In order to solve a puzzle we need to unravel the complexities and uncertainties that are preventing us from finding the correct answer. Puzzles are solved by detective work.

We must recognize that there is a correct answer and that it is possible to find that answer. An example makes the point. The wreck of the *Titanic* lay somewhere on the seabed of the Atlantic Ocean for many years. No one was able to pinpoint the exact location. Then a team of researchers studied the last radio signals, computed distances and, with new deep sea surveillance equipment, began a search which eventually found the hulk of the

*Titanic.* This puzzle, like so many others, was only solved when a team of persistent experts with suitable equipment dedicated themselves to the project.

Puzzles fall into three broad categories: soluble, currently insoluble, and insoluble. In the case of a soluble puzzle, the answer can be found with existing knowledge. The solution simply requires the relevant detective work. For example, the number of minutes of Louis XVI's life could be calculated. The exact moment of his birth was recorded as was the moment of his death. All the rest is a matter of mathematics.

In the case of currently insoluble puzzles, the answer is theoretically capable of being discovered, but we lack one or more pieces of the jigsaw. In science such puzzles occur all the time. In the late 1970s Dr Robin Baker, a zoologist at Manchester University, found that blindfolded subjects taken to a secret destination could often correctly point to home.[2] How? Baker did not know, but he experimented by fixing a bar magnet to the subjects' foreheads. Baker discovered that the capacity to determine direction was destroyed once the earth's magnetic field was disturbed. The puzzle was solved; human beings can orientate themselves to the earth's magnetic field.

Some puzzles are likely to be insoluble forever. Who was Jack the Ripper? We will never know for sure: the puzzle cannot be solved. Those who knew the identity of the killer have died without giving up their secret and there is no way that the missing jigsaw pieces can be found.

## DILEMMAS

Some situations are dilemmas – it is difficult to choose the best solution or determine what is the right thing to do. Even with all the available information, there is no way to be certain that your judgement is correct.

The most important thing about a dilemma is that there are at least two options for action that are virtually equally attractive or unattractive; the full merits of each cannot be known without going ahead in time. People talk about being 'stuck on the horns of a dilemma'. This is an apt analogy. A dilemma cannot be resolved by a computer programme: it requires human judgement.

Perhaps the most intractable dilemmas have a moral aspect: a chemical company can make extraordinary profits but only at the cost of causing untraceable pollution in the local river. What should they do? A manager wants to fire a long-serving employee who has been strange and depressed since he suffered a motorcycle accident. What should the manager do? These are, in essence, questions concerning human values and no additional facts will assist in solving these dilemmas.

## DEFINING YOUR PROJECT

We must realize that mysteries, assignments, difficulties, opportunities, puzzles, and dilemmas require specialized analytical procedures (described in the first four steps of TOSIDPAR). There is a real risk that if we call everything difficult a 'problem', we will not solve it.

Throughout the rest of this book you will work through a project – a real mystery, assignment, difficulty, opportunity, puzzle, or dilemma. This allows you to interact with the ideas in this book and learn the stances and skills used by effective managers. First, you need to define the issue that you are going to work on. Here are the rules:

1   *You must own the issue.* The solution must be either directly or indirectly within your personal influence. It is useless to take an issue like bringing peace to Northern Ireland or eliminating the global greenhouse effect unless you are directly concerned. Choose something within your own world.

2   *The best solution must be obscure.* Avoid selecting an issue that is too simple or essentially straightforward.

3   *Select an issue that is probably soluble.* Try not to choose something that is almost certain to fail. Even if you are a police officer in East London, do not choose to unravel the Jack the Ripper mystery; the chances of success are too slim.

4   *Choose an issue that is the right scale for learning.* For your first trial do not select a huge challenge that will take months or years to complete. Remember that you are learning. Select an issue that could be resolved in no more than two months.

5   *Ensure that you are personally committed to finding a solution.* Do not select an issue unless you personally care about finding

an effective answer. If your heart is not in the process you will lack the necessary commitment.

6   *Try to involve others.* Learning is more likely to be effective if the practical work takes place in a group setting. Therefore, it makes sense to pick an issue that several people can work through at the same time.

7   *Choose a work issue if possible.* The wording of questions in this book makes it especially suitable for work-based issues although, with imagination, any 'problem' can be used.

The following eight chapters deal with the TOSIDPAR approach. At the end of each chapter you should undertake the next step of your project. A word of warning: do not begin working on your project until you reach the special section at the end of the chapter. The project work duplicates the logic of the chapter and it is unnecessary to use the tools twice.

## YOUR PROJECT

The first step is to chose a suitable topic. Consider all of the issues that you face at the present time. Think widely; consider all your work problems (or home life if you are willing to adapt any inappropriate questions in the text). List the possible issues below.

*Possible issues:*

a

b

c

d

e

Now pick the issue that meets the following criteria and write a description below:

1   You own the issue.

2   The best solution is obscure.

3   The issue is probably soluble.

4   The issue is the right scale for learning.

5   You are personally committed to finding a solution.

*The issue I want to work on is:*

*The reasons that I have chosen this issue are:*

a

b

c

# 4 *Step one*
# *Tuning in*

The first of the eight steps for structured problem solving is the 'T' in TOSIDPAR, and this stands for tuning in. The expression 'tuning in' is borrowed from music where it refers to the initial phase of a performance in which each musician tunes his or her instrument to the particular demands of the next piece to be played. That is exactly what capable problem solvers do.

The importance of tuning in has been recognized for many generations. In approximately 490 BC Sun Tzu, a Chinese general, wrote a book called *The Art of War.*[1] He wrote, 'Spies are the most important element in war, because on them depends an army's ability to move' and 'what enables the wise sovereign and the good general to strike and conquer, and to achieve things beyond the reach of ordinary men, is foreknowlege'. Many years later the great General Wellington said, 'Time spent in reconnaissance is never wasted'.

Whenever we detect a problem, the first thing that must be done is to define it as a separate event – a distinct project. All too often we fail to be effective because everything blurs into the background. When nothing is distinct, no effective action can be taken.

Tuning in requires receptivity. Often the greatest enemy to objectivity is the person who stares back when we look in a mirror. In order to explain this we require an understanding of the psychological phenomenon of 'mind sets'. In essence the idea is simple: we all have our own personal philosophy for understanding the world and ascribing meanings to what we see.

Different people have different mind sets. This point was made beautifully by Ramakrishna in his story of a group of blind men encountering an elephant for the first time. Each blind man

approached the elephant: the one who grasped the leg said, 'The
elephant is like a pillar'. The man who held an ear said, 'No, the
elephant is like a fan'. Another man stretched out and touched the
tail and said, 'You are both wrong, an elephant is like a rope'.

The skills of active listening are essential to tuning in. Active
listening requires definite commitment and personal discipline.
The listener has deliberately to prepare himself to listen. Perhaps
the chief requirement is to 'have room' for the situation and the
other people involved. If we are preoccupied with our own
thoughts and feelings, we are not available to be receptive.

When listening it is helpful to try to understand the other
person's views without superimposing your own views or judgements prematurely. One way to prevent effective tuning in is to
jump in with your own viewpoint before the other people involved
have been able to express their point fully.

Active listening shows others that you respect and value their
contribution. The differences between people offer a resource for
progress.

## TOOLBOX: ACTIVE LISTENING

| | |
|---|---|
| Try using the following behaviours whilst meeting with others: | |
| *Checking* | Repeating what has been said to check your own understanding |
| *Clarifying* | Putting others' points in your own words |
| *Supporting* | Showing interest; wanting to know how the other person thinks |
| *Effective delivery* | Clear, logical, concise presentation |
| *Being specific* | Avoiding vague generalizations |
| *Avoiding repetition* | Making points once only |
| *Giving thought* | Pausing before replying |

Tuning in puts issues into context. It is important to understand all
the relevant factors within which a problem occurs. For example,

the law-abiding visitor to the United States may find it important to know that:

■ In Indiana it is illegal to ride on a bus within four hours of eating garlic.
■ In Nebraska a barber is breaking the law if he eats onions between the hours of 7:00 am and 7:00 pm.
■ In Wisconsin a pet elephant must be kept on a lead when taken for a walk in a public street.
■ In South Carolina it is illegal to drink water in a bar.

Context can be vitally important. A slight cut on the finger is a trivial event for most people but a life-threatening accident to a haemophiliac. Understanding the context in which a problem occurs enables the meaning to become apparent. It is interesting to note that great leaders spend a great deal of effort tuning people in to situations.

## HOW TO TUNE IN

Tuning in has five stages:

| | | |
|---|---|---|
| 1 | Categorizing the problem | Answers the question: what sort of task is this? |
| 2 | Situation appraisal | Answers the question: what are the issues? |
| 3 | Significance analysis | Answers the question: what is important? |
| 4 | Getting organized | Answers the question: how can we work on this problem effectively? |
| 5 | Emotional tuning in | Answers the question: how can we work on this problem with energy? |

## Categorizing the problem

The first stage in tuning in determines whether we are confronted with a mystery, assignment, difficulty, opportunity, puzzle, or dilemma (or a mixture of these). The definitions are explored in the previous chapter, but we will briefly review them below.

*Mysteries* are 'unexplained deviations from what is expected'.

This definition emphasizes the word 'unexplained'. If something is happening that is different from our expectations and we don't know the reason, we have a mystery.

*Assignments* are usually obvious: someone in authority comes along and says to you, 'There is a job I want you to do'. You have been given an assignment. An assignment may be clear or vague, possible or impossible, mandatory or negotiable. It is in the nature of an assignment that you have an obligation to complete the task, although usually you can discuss the assignment and arrive at a 'psychological contract' with the assignor.

*Difficulties* are situations in which we know what needs to be done but the execution is demanding, exacting, or intricate. Difficulties can be subjective (in your own mind) or objective (real difficulties that most people would find challenging).

*Opportunities* are chances to do something differently or better: they can either be created or happen through fortune and luck.

*Puzzles* are situations in which there is a correct answer but we do not know what it is. To solve a puzzle we need to unravel complexities and uncertainties.

*Dilemmas* are issues in which it is difficult to choose the best solution or determine what is the right thing to do. You can never be certain that your judgement is correct. At least two options for action co-exist which are equally attractive and the full merits of which cannot be known.

Once we have categorized the 'problem' there is an important activity to be undertaken: we must categorize the task. For example, one task may require a vast amount of planning whilst another will require extensive information collection. As you become more familiar with the TOSIDPAR approach you will be able graphically to predict the likely challenges of each new task.

Consider two real-life examples. The first concerns a manager who has been given the task of co-ordinating a move of office location for 150 staff. The second example concerns a board of trustees of an international children's charity who are seeking to redefine their strategy. The people involved drew out the TOSIDPAR process (see the figure opposite), giving a larger box to the more challenging steps. We can see that each task requires a quite different approach.

## Two examples of the TOSIDPAR process

*Planning an office move*       *Establishing a new strategy for a children's charity*

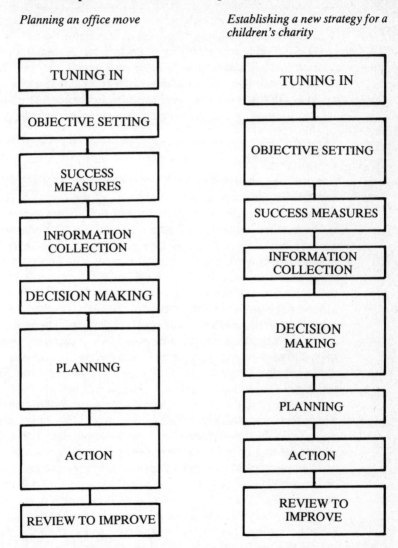

In the example of planning an office move, the most challenging steps are planning and action whereas in the second example, the children's charity, the most challenging steps are objective setting, decision making, and review to improve.

## TOOLBOX: CATEGORIZING THE TASK

> Consider the task that you are about to undertake and identify the challenges of each remaining step of the TOSIDPAR approach. Rate each step in terms of the expected difficulty (on a 1–10 scale) and the estimated importance (on a 1–10 scale). On a flip chart draw out the TOSIDPAR process as a series of boxes and ensure that the size of each box approximately represents the challenge of that step.

### Situation appraisal

Situation appraisal requires that all the existing facts are gathered and turned into a meaningful assessment of the situation. Assume that you are on a light aircraft crossing the Sonora desert in the south-west United States and your plane crashes. The pilot is killed, and the aircraft burnt out. Before you can begin to think about how to overcome the difficulties you face, it is necessary to ask many questions. How hot is it? How hot will it become? What are the chances that someone will come to look for you? Where is the nearest habitation? Are you physically fit? What is the best advice available for those who become lost in deserts? These are just a few of the questions that must be asked by the survivors as part of their situation appraisal. The more effectively such questions are answered, the stronger will be the platform of understanding on which the rest of the TOSIDPAR process will be built.

Capable problem solvers adopt an outward-looking approach when they undertake a situation appraisal. The importance of doing this becomes clear through an example. I became a consultant to a design team responsible for putting together a new concept in office automation. They had seventy engineers working on the project and were spending $8 million a year on research and development. At our first meeting it became apparent that morale was disastrously low and all of the executives privately feared that other companies were ahead in the race to launch an automated office. We tried to tune in by asking the question: what, exactly, are the competitors doing? But no one knew the answer; the topic had not been considered. An urgent competitor analysis programme was started. Two months later the data had been gathered and it was obvious that my client's company was about to launch an inferior and unproven product that would be priced 30 per cent higher than the competition. The project was abandoned at a cost to the parent company of $20 million. The main reason for failure, they later admitted, was an inadequate tuning in to the external environment.

Here are two simple techniques that enable us to begin situation appraisal. Ideally you will have bold pens and two different coloured packs of Post-it notes, but sheets of paper or a flip chart can be equally useful.

## TOOLBOX: STRUCTURED FACT FINDING

> This provides a framework to help us ask the right questions. The structured fact-finding technique can be used by an individual but it becomes much more powerful when used within a team. On the first colour Post-it notes, write down all the questions that you would like to have answered in relation to this situation. Do not think about the information that you have at the moment and write only one question on one note. When you are exhausted use a suitable flat surface on which to mount the completed Post-it notes, clustering together those questions that are similar.

## TOOLBOX: SITUATION ANALYSIS

> This process collects and organizes available information; it follows directly on from structured fact finding. Take the other coloured Post-it notes and write one item of information that you know about the situation on each. Try to answer each of the questions generated by the structured fact-finding process. Mount the completed Post-it notes on the surface under the questions. The situation analysis technique is even more valuable if it is undertaken as part of a group effort.

### Significance analysis

Significance analysis has a different purpose: it enables us to recognize what is relatively important. This process is vital because there is a tendency to spend one's time tackling urgent rather than important issues. Consider the plight of those people who were lost in the desert when their aircraft crashed. Is their situation serious? How important is it that the survivors come to the best solution? How urgent is the difficulty that they face? Answering such questions helps ensure that we focus on the most important issues.

## TOOLBOX: SIGNIFICANCE ANALYSIS

To address the significance of data gathered there are four key questions that should be addressed. It pays to write the answers down. The four questions are:

■ *Why* do we need to be concerned with this issue?

■ *How important* is the issue (judged in relation to the other things that require our attention)?

■ *Who* should be concerned with resolving the issue?

■ What are the *real constraints* or limitations that we face?

A flip chart can be prepared with four columns:

**Significance analysis chart**

| Why important? | How important? | Who concerned? | Real constraints |
|---|---|---|---|

## Getting organized

Early on in the tuning-in step we must begin to get organized. Without leadership and appropriate resources nothing constructive will happen. Leaders have particular responsibilities: they communicate the meaning of tasks and assignments to their team members. Various leadership styles can used. The most significant feature is the readiness of the followers in relation to the specific task in hand. In general, this advice holds good:[2]

## TOOLBOX: APPROPRIATE LEADERSHIP STYLE

Use the framework below to help you determine the appropriate leadership style to use. The framework will help you decide how much direction to impose and how much support to give.

STYLE 1: TELLING
If someone is unwilling and unable in relation to the task, you are advised to adopt a strict directive approach.

STYLE 2: SELLING
If someone is willing but unable in relation to the task, you are advised to adopt a supportive directive approach.

STYLE 3: PARTICIPATING
If someone is unwilling to take full responsibility but able in relation to the task, you are advised to adopt an empowering approach.

STYLE 4: DELEGATING
If someone is willing and able in relation to the task, you are advised to adopt a 'hands-off' approach.

Leaders must create the right environment for effective problem solving. This involves paying attention to two questions: who should be involved? And second, where should the process take place? The first issue – who should be involved – is vital. People with the skills to contribute and the power to make things happen must be included; otherwise nothing useful will emerge.

The importance of the second issue – where the process should take place – is often underestimated. The reality is that some environments are much more conducive than others. An example makes the point. A semiconductor manufacturer held a meeting of technical experts who had been trying in vain to come to a consensus on the future development of their products. They chose to meet in an elegant hotel. Well-worn differences of view were aired and eventually the leader said, 'It is clear that we must come to a decision. We will continue the debate in here, without interruption until a consensus has been achieved.' As time for lunch came and went without a break there was an inner pressure to come to a collective decision. Eventually an agreed development plan was determined. They broke at half past three for a celebration lunch, and returned about five o'clock to set objectives (a process that took much of the night). That meeting, which redirected the strategy of the company, could not have taken place in the office because the busy and familiar environment would have failed to give the necessary 'specialness' to the occasion.

## Emotional tuning in

We may wish that we were rational beings who tackle every issue with the cold logic of a computer working through algorithms. It is not possible. People, for better or worse, are affected by feelings – our emotions affect the quality of what we do and the gusto with which we do it. Tuning in has a psychological impact: it helps people feel good about the task that they are about to undertake. The Japanese understand this very well. They refuse to rush into things and take time to find consensus, harmony, and shared commitment.

The final stage of tuning in determines how we feel about the issue that confronts us. Emotional blockages erode effectiveness and need to be resolved. Time should be taken to explore openly any emotional barriers that are exposed by the questioning process described below.[3] There are five emotional tuning-in questions that it is worthwhile to ask.

■ Do all those involved really want to win and overcome all challenges? If not, why not?

■ Do all those involved feel that they will gain real benefit from winning?

■ Does the task offer all those involved a chance to overcome obstacles, demonstrate superior prowess, and do things that other people find difficult?

■ Do all those involved have the experience or brainpower available to approach the task?

■ Are all those involved willing to tolerate uncertainty or ambiguity?

Answering these five questions helps explore the emotional underworld that affects the way that we solve problems. From time to time, it is vital to take stock of the non-rational factors that influence so many aspects of our effectiveness.

## TUNING-IN SKILLS AUDIT

Tuning in requires distinct skills. These are explored above, but it is important to relate the skills to yourself. Answer the following questions to audit your own skills.

1   How are your attitudes and value judgements likely to affect your judgement? Give examples.

2   How do you avoid jumping to premature conclusions? Give examples.

3   Are you a skilful listener? In what situations does your listening fail? Give examples.

4   Do you ensure that you have gathered an effective team to tackle the situation in hand? How do you develop teams? Give examples.

5    Do you systematically appraise situations in order to ask the right questions? How? Give examples.

6    How do you effectively prioritize tasks in order of importance and urgency? Give examples.

7    How skilful are you at tuning in others to the task in hand? Give examples.

## YOUR PROJECT

In Chapter 3 you selected the issue that you wanted to work on for the rest of this book. Tune in by answering the questions below:

1    Is your issue primarily a mystery, an assignment, a difficulty, an opportunity, a puzzle, or a dilemma?

2    Consider the task that you are about to undertake and identify the challenges of each remaining step of the TOSIDPAR approach. On a separate sheet of paper, rate each step in terms of the expected difficulty (on a 1–10 scale) and the estimated importance (on a 1–10 scale). Draw out the TOSIDPAR process as a series of boxes and ensure that the size of each box approximately represents the challenge of that step. See the example on page 27.)

3    What questions do you need to ask to tune in to the issue? Use the technique of structured fact finding as described on page 29. List the questions below.

4    What do you know about the issue now? Use the technique of situation analysis as described on page 29. List the information below.

5    How important is the issue? Use the technique of significance analysis as shown below.

| *Why important?* | *How important?* | *Who concerned?* | *Real constraints* |
| --- | --- | --- | --- |

6   How do you feel about the issue? Use the five emotional
     tuning-in questions listed below.

     a   How are your attitudes and value judgements likely to
          affect your judgement in relation to this issue?

     b   How do you avoid jumping to premature conclusions in
          relation to this issue?

     c   Have you listened to other people's views in relation to
          this issue?

     d   If it is appropriate, have you gathered an effective team to
          tackle this issue?

     e   Have you tuned in the other people involved to the issue
          that you are working on?

# 5  *Step two*
   *Objective setting*

This second step of the structured approach provides focus and direction. Objective setting clarifies, as precisely as possible, the desired outcomes from the activities we are about to undertake.

Objectives are tangible expressions of a 'compelling vision', which is the essence of leadership.[1] Outstandingly successful managers, army generals, teachers, or parents articulate an integrated set of objectives, which like a tapestry, weaves a vivid description or vision of how the future can and should be. Then leaders convince others to help make this vision become a reality. The effective communication of a coherent set of valid and achievable objectives is the most important task of management.

Each individual in the organization needs to become enrolled in the corporate objectives and gain something of personal worth as the organization achieves its goals. Objectives that attract people are based on deeper values than mere profitability and commercial advantage. Managers need to think about the values that underlie their objectives.[2] The aim is to set objectives that benefit all the stakeholders in the organization.

In fact, all objectives are based on values – what we believe to be good or bad, important or not important. Values determine behaviour. Managements are unfocused without a coherent value system. Values have to be known, consistent, practised, and honoured. Leaders with clear values attract others towards them, thereby enabling the organization to develop a consensus about what is good or bad, important or not important.

Clarifying values should be undertaken systematically. Inner beliefs are more important than external analysis.

A clarified value meets six conditions. These are:

1   *Values have to be chosen from alternatives.* Values that have been positively chosen will be firmly held. Choosing strengthens commitment. Confrontation and debate are essential to eliminating unacceptable values.
2   *Values have to be consistent with each other.* Values must support each other. We should all check that the values we live by are intellectually consistent.
3   *Core values need to be few in number.* Trying to adopt an excessive number of core values dissipates effort and is confusing.
4   *Values need to be actionable.* A value that cannot be put into effect becomes a weakness: only when we are convinced that we can uphold the value in all eventualities should it be adopted.
5   *Values must be attractive.* People need to be able to be uplifted by values. It must be possible for most people to feel pride when playing a part in making a value become a reality.
6   *Values need to be capable of being communicated.* A key leadership task is translating values into terms that are meaningful to each individual.

The relationship between values and objectives becomes clearer as we consider an example. In the 1980s Prince Charles deepened his interest in architecture, and became concerned about the inhuman design of new buildings. He said that architects and town planners had destroyed much that was good and replaced it with self-aggrandizing and ugly buildings which offended the natural harmony of mankind's spirit. Of course, there was an outcry from the architectural establishment but Prince Charles's views attracted great popular support. More and more architects began to support the values of 'community architecture' and their objectives changed. New objectives promoted human-scale designs, private space for everyone, and a return to the English tradition of decoration.

Clarified values shape objectives and provide managers with a 'mission'. The root of 'mission' is *mittere*, which is the Latin verb meaning 'to send'. A missionary goes forth to preach the faith. Corporate objectives have the same purpose: they enable managers to animate and guide people. Hope and conviction are as essential as logic and analysis in the formulation of objectives.

Objectives should be powerful statements about what managers really believe. People are persuaded by actions rather than words. Objectives are, therefore, communications: their symbolic meaning is profound. Objectives provide the raw material for the creation of organizational stories, myths, and legends.

It is difficult to put the principle into practice. People often prefer to get into action (which is concrete), rather than devote their efforts to clarifying objectives (which are visionary).

Objectives provide a framework for information collection and decision making. Objectives are definitions of the desired outcome (but not the means of accomplishment). An objective is like the beam of a torch on a dark night: it shows us the way to go.

Once we have clear and understood objectives, all our endeavour can be focused towards achievement. Objectives are the primary tools for directing and integrating human effort.

## HOW TO SET OBJECTIVES

Objective setting has four stages:

| | | |
|---|---|---|
| 1 | Establishing possible objectives | Answers the question: what could we aim towards? |
| 2 | Choosing the objective(s) | Answers the question: what should we aim towards? |
| 3 | Elaborating the objective(s) | Answers the question: what are the implications of our choice? |
| 4 | Communicating the objective(s) | Answers the question: how can we enrol others? |

### Establishing possible objectives

You will recall that there are six variations of the 'problem': mysteries, assignments, difficulties, opportunities, puzzles, and dilemmas. The objective-setting process is different in each case and we will explore the distinctions below.

**Mystery solving**
Setting objectives for mystery solving is often relatively straight-forward. Something is going wrong. We need to know the causes of the unexplained deviation. Once we know the reasons why something is going wrong, we no longer have a mystery. Thus the objective is always to find the real causes for the deviation.

**Assignments**
The distinctive feature of assignments is that the objectives are set by someone else. The assignee has to ensure that he or she really understands the purpose of the task and the relevant constraints. A 'contract', which is an explicit agreement as to the responsibilities of both sides, is essential.

Resource availability, time frames, and success criteria are the most important issues. The connection or linkage between the assignment and other tasks within the organization needs to be understood. The efficiency of these linkages can make all the difference between success and failure.

When assignments are given without reference to broader objectives, the inevitable result is fragmentation and wasted effort. For example, the management services team of an international manufacturing company undertook the task of developing a computer system to automate order intake and product tracking. They worked for nearly two years and produced a state-of-the-art proposal, only to be told by the chief executive that 'the key criterion is cost. We want an adequate system as cheaply as possible.' The team scrapped their work and went back to first principles.

**Difficulties**
Difficulties are situations in which we know what needs to be done but the execution is demanding, exacting, or intricate. Either we do not know how to manage the situation or feel that we lack adequate resources.

Setting the objective for overcoming difficulties is usually relatively straightforward. The objective is always to overcome as many of the difficulties as cheaply as possible. This is true for both subjective and objective difficulties (if you have forgotten the distinction between subjective and objective difficulties, refer back to page 16).

## Opportunities

Opportunities are sources of potential benefit. Objective setting in relation to seizing opportunities can be complex. We need objectives in three areas:

1 To define what opportunities we are seeking to create.
2 To gather the necessary intelligence so that we can detect opportunities as they occur.
3 To evaluate opportunities rapidly and move quickly to exploit those that seem promising.

Although opportunism is often seen as a personal characteristic, the quintessence of the entrepreneur's spirit, it is possible to build opportunism into a corporate culture.

## Puzzles

Situations in which there is only a limited number of correct answers are puzzles. In such cases the broad objective is always the same: to find the correct solution. But there can be many specific sub-objectives, each helping to unravel the complexities and uncertainties that are preventing us from finding the correct answer.

## Dilemmas

Dilemmas arise when a decision must be made but either it is difficult to choose the best solution or to determine what is the right thing to do. There are always at least two options for action that may be virtually equally attractive but the full merits of each cannot be known without going ahead in time.

Resolving dilemmas requires human judgement. For example, in the early 1980s the Proctor and Gamble company in Europe faced a dilemma: should they launch a liquid washing agent code-named Vizir? The product had not passed the stringent P & G test programme but there were signs that a competitor was ready to launch Lisp, a rival product. It was known that the first product launched would gain significant marketing advantages, but would it be right to short-circuit the tried and tested P & G product development process? Added to this question was a further dimension: P & G was, at the time, organized on a geographical basis. Should this organizational concept be changed as the differences between European countries lessened? If so, was Vizir the right platform on which to build a new European organizational structure?

The broad objective in such cases is always the same: to take a decision that provides the greatest advantage with the fewest disadvantages. But the specific objectives must always be teased out from a complex web of truth, half-truth, and uncertainty. Principles, values, strategies, and hunches are as relevant as facts and hard data. Those engaged in resolving dilemmas are well advised to carefully consider their objectives; this provides the essential basis for taking a wise decision.

## TOOLBOX: GENERATING POSSIBLE OBJECTIVES

> Either on a flip chart or on Post-it notes, generate as many possible objectives as possible. Use a brainstorming technique with a team if you can. List all possible objectives and refine them so that they are clear and distinct. Eliminate overlaps and combine similar suggestions. Make a list of all the possible objectives without evaluation.

### Choosing the objective(s)

We now have a list of possible objectives and must choose which to adopt. Sometimes there is no argument. Imagine, for example, that you are in a car accident and end up hanging over a precipice like a character from a Charlie Chaplin movie. The objective is simple: to reach safety.

In other situations the objectives are much more obscure. For example, a local government agency is contemplating closing a long-stay mental home and moving the inmates into the community. There are therapeutic arguments for doing this as it will prevent patients from being institutionalized, but there are also therapeutic hazards in moving disabled people into closer contact with the community. There are also responsibilities towards the local population to think about: it is possible that some of the patients may be dangerous. Add to this the activities of local pressure groups, the lack of community care workers, government policy, the views of the local newspaper, and the cost implications and it is difficult to establish the best objectives to follow.

Choosing an objective is a form of decision making. In complicated situations like the one above you are advised to use the full TOSIDPAR approach in order to establish relevant objectives. In other words, you will need to answer the question: what would success be? You must also collect relevant information, identify options, establish assessment criteria, make a decision, plan how this could be implemented, and so on. In particular, the distinction between essential and desirable characteristics, explored in the Decision steps (Chapter 8), can be very helpful. The problem solver loops through a mini-TOSIDPAR cycle in order to complete a single step.

In less complicated situations the objective(s) can be established with a simpler method. The benefits and drawbacks matrix has proved useful on many occasions.

## TOOLBOX: BENEFITS AND DRAWBACKS MATRIX

Complete the matrix below by listing possible objectives in the left-hand column and evaluating their benefits and drawbacks as shown. Allocate an importance rating (a score of 1–10 is usually satisfactory). If you are working with others it is helpful to draw the benefits and drawbacks matrix on a flip chart.

| *Objectives* | *Benefits* | *Drawbacks* | *Importance rating* |
| --- | --- | --- | --- |

## Elaborating the objective(s)

Objectives vary in their degree of specificity. The notion that some objectives are more specific than others is very practical. One of the most useful management tools – the tiers of objectives technique – was created from this idea. Let us explore the concept further.

Some objectives are expressed in very broad terms: for example, 'to provide an efficient city police force'. Other objectives are extremely specific: for example, 'to wheel-clamp fifteen cars in Police Division Q within the next hour'. To make matters more complicated, there are intermediate objectives, for example, 'to enable traffic to move through the city at an average speed of 15 miles an hour for 23 hours per day'.

Objectives have two dimensions: scale and time frame. Objectives can be broad in one or both of these dimensions. An example of an objective that is broad in scale is 'to decrease the amount of CFC gases used globally by 20 per cent in 12 months'. An objective that is narrow in scope but broad in time frame is for an 18-year-old medical student 'to become a brain surgeon'. An example of an objective that is broad along both dimensions (scale and time) is 'to develop the deserts of western China into the world's largest oil field by 2030'.

The two dimensions concept is illustrated in the figure below.

**Objectives can be broad in both scope and time frame**

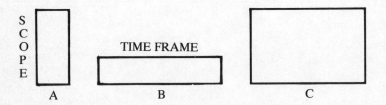

In the figure, A represents an objective that has broad scope but a narrow time frame (reducing the global emission of CFC gases over the next 12 months). B represents the opposite: an objective with a broad time frame but narrow scope (becoming a brain surgeon). C represents an objective that is broad on both dimensions (developing the oil reserves in western China).

Why is this distinction important? The reason is that the scale of the task, and therefore the resourcing implications, are greatly affected. I may have a broad objective to learn the Chinese language but this has few resourcing implications: I just require a few books, a tutor, and lots of time. However, if the objective is broad in scope, the resourcing implications can be vast. If I were given the task of building a space station on Mars, the scope of the task is gigantic; the resourcing implications are colossal.

However, a broad objective gives too general an overview to establish precisely what needs to be done. Therefore, specific objectives are required to enable everyone to visualize clearly their tasks. This is done by identifying the tiers or levels of objectives.

Between broad and specific objectives there are several intermediate levels which must be logically explored. This is done with the technique of tiers of objectives.

## TOOLBOX: TIERS OF OBJECTIVES

An example illustrates the technique of tiers of objectives. Let us assume that I have the broad objective, 'to complete this book three months from today'. I wish to identify the specific objectives that will provide me with an outline action plan. I proceed as follows: I write the broad objective on the top of a sheet of paper and ask the question: how will I achieve this? I generate as many options as I can and express these as objectives. Are they now sufficiently specific? If not, I take each one and ask the question again: how will I achieve this? Eventually, I will find that a network of objectives results in the shape of a pyramid. At the top are the broad overall objectives. At the base of the pyramid are the specific objectives that lead to definite and clearly focused action programmes.

### A sample tiers of objectives diagram

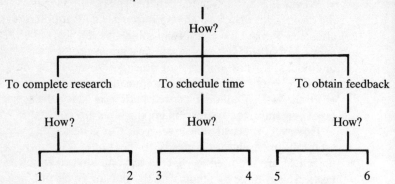

From this analysis six specific objectives were identified:

1   To hire an extra temporary research assistant immediately.
2   To buy a suitable statistical computer programme.
3   To cancel a two-week holiday planned for the next month!
4   To postpone a series of planned lectures.
5   To submit the draft manuscript to a panel of expert management teachers within the next two weeks.
6   To submit the draft manuscript to at least twenty managers and other professional workers within the next two weeks.

These six specific objectives provide much more focus and clarity than the single broad objective. If I had not used the tiers of objectives technique there was a risk that these detailed tasks would not have been identified.

But before we move on, there is a further step. I call it 'the necessary and sufficient test'.

## TOOLBOX: THE NECESSARY AND SUFFICIENT TEST

> Two questions need to be asked: first, are all the actions necessary? Second, taken together, do we believe that the actions identified are sufficient to achieve the. broad objective?

I look at the six specific objectives shown in the sample and ask: are they all necessary? I conclude that I do not really need the new computer programme; the new research assistant can do the necessary calculations using the existing computing facilities. I also decide that it is not necessary to cancel the planned holiday; it will be sufficient to postpone it.

I then ask the second question: do I believe that the actions are sufficient to achieve my broad objective? The answer is 'no'. Since writing a book is a task that requires uninterrupted concentration, I must share my difficulty with my colleagues and family to negotiate enough space to finish the project.

Having undertaken the necessary and sufficient test I now have these revised specific objectives:

1   To hire an additional temporary research assistant immediately.
2   To discuss with friends, family members, and colleagues how I can gain their support in helping me with my writing task.
3   To postpone a planned two-week holiday.
4   To postpone a series of planned lectures.
5   To submit the draft manuscript to a panel of expert management teachers within the next two weeks.
6   To submit the draft manuscript to at least twenty managers and other professional workers within the next two weeks.

In the TOSIDPAR structured approach, each of these specific objectives is considered as a distinct project to be processed separately. It is often necessary to revert to tuning in for each specific objective so that it can be fully addressed.

Several objectives may be pursued at the same time. We should seek to identify all current objectives and reduce overlap or conflict. For example, I have two objectives at the moment. One is to lose ten pounds in weight, and the second is to complete this manuscript by the due date. Unlikely as it may appear, it is possible to pursue both of the objectives at the same time. As I type this paragraph I am sitting in my room in a health resort, having just eaten a salad lunch and about to attend an aerobics class. 'Killing two birds with one stone' is the aim. The concept of harmonizing objectives, sometimes called 'duelling', is practised by many effective people.

When we consider how to elaborate objectives there is another issue that needs to be discussed. Managers are accustomed to 'output' objectives: these state what should be achieved in measurable terms. 'Competence' objectives are less well understood but equally important. They are set by asking the question: what do we need to be good at in order to achieve our output objectives? Competence objectives focus our minds on the strengths we need to create.

Output and competence objectives go hand in hand; they support each other. For example, a high-performance sports car manufacturer sets an output objective to sell 10,000 cars per annum. This can only be achieved if the sports cars are high quality, reliable, well designed, and competitively priced. To achieve the output objective the organization has to set competence objectives in relation to high quality, design excellence, and efficiency.

We pull together all the objectives into a convenient package using the 'from–to statement' technique. This is described in the toolbox below.

## TOOLBOX: FROM–TO STATEMENT TECHNIQUE

Review all the work you have done in elaborating your objectives and ask what you wish to move from; enter this in the first column. Then identify what you want to move to and enter the elements in the second column. Be as specific as possible.

*From*                          *To*

## Communicating the objectives

Objectives are vital because they enable our endeavours to be focused towards achievement. Objectives are tools for directing and integrating human effort. This implies that objectives must clearly communicate and that others must dedicate themselves to their achievement.

Objectives should be elaborated in a vision that is instilled in everyone who can help transform the objective into reality. Objectives must become compelling.

Persuasion is needed to shape, reinforce, and change attitudes. From management's viewpoint, the main purpose of persuasion is to generate a willing climate that supports managerial objectives. If such willingness does not exist, the whole fabric of the organization breaks down. Once destroyed, it can take years, even decades, for willingness to be rebuilt.

Managers cannot assume that their staff are dullards who will be seduced by an attractive presentation. People are persuaded when they feel that ideas are expressed by someone with integrity.

## TOOLBOX: COMMUNICATING OBJECTIVES

Use the following checklist before you attempt to persuade others to your point of view.

1 When you appoint new staff, do you select those who support your objectives?
2 Do you use training as a technique for indoctrinating the importance of objectives into subordinates?
3 How effectively do you remove, weaken, or displace those who are influential in leading people against your objectives?
4 Do you explain objectives in small group discussions which are expertly led and guide people towards the views you want them to hold?
5 Have you developed your image as a 'parent figure' in whom people feel trust and to whom they give their loyalty?
6 Do you reward conformity so that people are motivated to commit themselves to your objectives?

> 7  Do you avoid over-dramatic presentations of objectives, which are often discounted or ignored?
> 8  How effectively do you warn of the consequences of non-acceptance of your objectives?
> 9  Do you keep repeating your message so that it is heard time and time again?
> 10  Do you try to distill the essence of your objective and put it across clearly?

Persuasion is needed to give broad objectives their compelling quality. This force strengthens the heart of the organization. Everyone in the organization then uses the broad objectives to set priorities and schedules, and allocate resources. Unless objectives are shared, the organization will drift whilst others, driven by clearer objectives, gain the competitive advantage.

There is a wonderful story which makes the point. In the twelfth century a passerby saw two men at work on a building site. He called out, 'What are you doing?' The first man looked up and said in a weary voice, 'I'm laying bricks', but the other man's eyes were full of sparkle as he said, 'I am building a cathedral'.

The objective-setting stage is complete when there is a full and clear definition of what is to be achieved – which is understood by all who can contribute. It is helpful to review objectives regularly to see whether they are still valid.

## OBJECTIVE-SETTING SKILLS AUDIT

Objective setting requires distinct skills including visualizing, generating, choosing, 'tiering' (using the tiers of objectives technique), and communicating. These are explored above, but it is important to relate the skills to yourself. Answer the following questions to audit your own skills.

1  How much time do you consciously set aside to think about the future?

2    Do you have a clear vision of what you are trying to achieve in your job? What is it?

3    Do you have a clear vision of what you are trying to achieve in your career? What is it?

4    Do you set broad objectives for your major activities in your job? What are they?

5    Do you logically map out all of the specific objectives that follow from the broad objectives?

6    How do you know whether you effectively communicate your objectives to others?

7    How do you know whether you effectively persuade others that your objectives are worthwhile?

## YOUR PROJECT

In the previous chapter you tuned in to the issue that you wanted to work on for the rest of this book. Set your objectives by answering the questions below:

1   What are the possible objectives that you could have? (Use the 'Generating possible objectives' tool.) List the possibilities below.

2  What values are you pursuing? List below.

3  Look at each of these values and ask yourself: are these really clear? Use the checklist below. Write your answers on a separate sheet of paper.
   a   Has the value been chosen from alternatives?
   b   Is the value consistent with your other values?
   c   Have you a few core values?
   d   Are your values actionable?
   e   Is the value attractive to you (and others)?
   f   Are your values capable of being communicated?

4  What objectives will you adopt? (Try using the benefits and drawbacks matrix or a TOSIDPAR mini-loop described on page 43.)

5  What are your specific objectives? (Use the tiers of objectives approach and the necessary and sufficient test described on pages 45–6. Go as far as you can.)

6 What changes are needed/wanted?

| *From* | *To* |
| --- | --- |
| | |

7 What do you have to be good at to achieve your broad objectives?

8 What time frame can be put upon this objective?

9 How can you get everyone involved to fully understand the objective?

10 Do you have other objectives that may conflict? What are they?

# 6 *Step three*
# *Success measurement*

Success measurement establishes, as precisely as possible, standards against which performance will be judged. It gives measuring rods to guide activities. Without success measures, there is no possibility of reviewing performance.

Many people don't set success criteria or establish how they will measure success. It is difficult to know why we are so resistant to measurement; perhaps because of a dislike of being tied down or a mistrust of quantitative approaches. However, whether we like it or not, the absence of success measurement is almost always a fault. Many successful managers emphasize that measurement is the single most important activity that can be undertaken.

Some theoretical background may be of interest. The TOSIDPAR structured approach owes much to a branch of physics known as systems theory. One of the most important principles is that a feedback loop must be built into every system. In order for a car to be driven within speed limits the driver must get constant real-time feedback on the current speed: this is, of course, done through the speedometer. The intelligence of the system is directly affected by the quality of feedback information available.

A clothing company called Benetton has taken the feedback loop principle to heart and made it into a source of competitive advantage. Sophisticated computers constantly monitor buying trends and changing patterns of demand are quickly identified. Dedicated factories change their manufacturing plans in an almost unbelievably short time. Distribution is fast and efficient. The result is a total business system that responds quickly to feedback and, largely because of this, Benetton has become a household name in many countries around the world.

Many managers tend to measure straightforward activities only. Their department's expenditure on telephone calls will be known to the nearest decimal point. But consider, for example, a vital topic: presentation skills. How many times will a manager deliberately collect comprehensive feedback on the effectiveness of his or her presentations? Many managers have not yet fully learned the importance of measurement.

Thomas Taylor is a shopkeeper. He judges his overall performance by looking at the weekly takings. However, he has other objectives and he finds it more difficult to measure the performance of these. Thomas wants his staff to be especially polite with customers. How will he measure whether this objective is being achieved totally, in part, or not at all? Thomas may decide to interview a random sample of, say, fifty customers each month, and ask them to rate the quality of service in his shop. This will give him feedback about the 'politeness level' of his staff. When the results of the survey are graphed, Thomas has the basis for knowing how well he is doing on the politeness objective.

What Thomas had to do was to stand back and ask himself: 'how am I going to obtain feedback on the performance of my shop in relation to all the specific objectives that I have?' Only with this data available can appropriate remedial action be undertaken.

A good example of success measures is found included in objectives for the Spanish railway system. In 1984, 3.2 billion pesetas was given by the Spanish government to make the trains run on time. The Spanish Ministry of Transport insisted that 'by 1986, 80 per cent of long-distance trains will arive at their destination less than ten minutes late. Average speeds are to be increased by 9 per cent and the workforce reduced by 5,130 jobs during the period.' Such precise success measures enable a realistic programme of improvement to be planned.

Managers are often confused by the terms 'success criteria' and 'success measures'. Success criteria refers to what you deem a success. Success measures refer to how you are going to track your progress. An example clarifies the difference between these two terms. Jane Jackson is a lady of middle years. She keeps quite active but too much sitting in the car, an occasional excess of gin-and-tonics, and plenty of good food has meant that she is not as fit as she wishes. She sets herself an objective to become fitter. Jane

decides that success would mean more than removing a few excess
bulges; her success criteria include being able to run 3 miles in
20 minutes, surviving a full aerobics class, and being able to swim
30 lengths of the pool. In order to measure her success she decides
to undertake a monthly test and record her progress. This becomes
easier to grasp when laid out as a table:

| Objective | Success criteria | Success measures |
|---|---|---|
| To get fitter | Run 3 miles in 20 minutes | Time trials conducted weekly |
| | Survive an aerobics class | Class attended and records kept |
| | Swim 30 lengths of the pool | Log kept of distances swum |

When you have a specific objective (as described in the previous
chapter) it will often have the rudiments of success criteria built in.
But it always pays to ask two questions: what precisely will I define
as success? And how will I measure my progress? Take the
example about writing this book that I used in the previous
chapter. You will remember that six specific objectives were identified. When I asked these questions – what precisely will I define as
success? and how will I measure my progress? – there were interesting results. The goals suddenly became clearer and more
tangible. The answers to the first question generated a mechanism
that provided feedback. It is useful to lay out this information as a
table.

Possibly I could have thought through all the elements listed
under success measures and success criteria without this step
but, in all honesty, I wouldn't have done so for two reasons.
Firstly, until questions have been asked the answers do not
appear, and second, many points of detail are lost unless they
are recorded.

**Elaborating objectives with success criteria and measures**

| Objectives | Success criteria | Success measures |
|---|---|---|
| 1 Hire research assistant | Working by Friday | Daily review |
| 2 Gain support from family, etc. | Each say that they will help | Checklist of all family members |
| 3 Postpone holiday | Book another within three months | Entry in diary of new dates |
| 4 Postpone lectures | Schedule for next term | Entry in diary of new dates |
| 5 Submit draft to teachers | Ten teachers asked to comment within one month | Checklist of teachers who can comment |
| 6 Submit draft to managers, etc. | Twenty managers asked to comment within one month | Checklist of managers who will comment |

# HOW TO SET SUCCESS MEASURES

Success measurement has three stages:

| | | |
|---|---|---|
| 1 | Establishing possible success criteria | Answers the question: what could we judge as successful? |
| 2 | Choosing success criteria | Answers the question: what should we judge as successful? |
| 3 | Identifying success measures | Answers the question: how will we measure progress? |

## Establishing possible success criteria

Some years ago an interesting experiment was performed into the nature of the achievement motivation in human beings. The subjects of the experiment were asked to take rubber rings and get them onto a short spike. They could choose the distance they stood from the spike. Some decided to stand close; others chose the opposite approach and retreated to a great distance. Interestingly, the subjects with the strongest achievement motivation were those who positioned themselves sufficiently far from the spike for there to be real challenge but not so far that the likelihood of failure became high.

Whenever success criteria are set, there has to be a decision as to the amount of stretch undertaken. Too little stretch will fail to motivate and mean that resources are wasted. Too much stretch overwhelms people and increases the likelihood of failure.

## TOOLBOX: GENERATING POSSIBLE SUCCESS CRITERIA

Either on a flip chart or on Post-it notes generate as many possible success criteria as possible. Use a brainstorming technique with a team if you can. List all possible success criteria and refine them so that they are clear and distinct. Eliminate overlaps and combine similar suggestions. Make a list of all the possible success criteria without evaluation.

### Choosing success criteria

All significant projects need to be broken down into 'bite-sized chunks' so that they can be tackled in a methodical and effective manner. Each bite-sized chunk needs its own success criterion, which is normally tracked by time. Following up the example I discussed earlier, the milestones for completing this book might be:

| Dates | Milestones |
| --- | --- |
| 1 September | Complete first draft |
| 7 September | Distribute drafts for criticism |
| 21 September | Collect all criticisms |
| 1 October | Complete list of all changes to be made |
| 21 October | Revised draft completed |
| 25 October | Revised draft submitted to the supervising editor |

Milestones make it possible to celebrate success. This has enormous potential benefits for morale. One manager said to me, 'In this company we have no habit of celebrating success. We take the view that "if a thing isn't a real success then it is a failure". I wonder if this has got anything to do with low motivation in the company?' This manager's instinct was right. Celebration of success has a great impact on motivation.

## TOOLBOX: STRETCH AND RELEVANCE MATRIX

Complete the matrix below by listing possible success criteria in the left-hand column and evaluating their stretch and relevance as shown. Use the following convention:

- A success criteria that puts you under maximum achievable stretch should be rated 0.
- A success criteria that puts you under severely excessive stretch should be rated +10.
- A success criteria that puts you under no significant stretch should be rated −10.
- A success criteria that is essential to achieving the established objectives should be rated 10.
- A success criteria that is irrelevant to achieving the established objectives should be rated 0.

If you are working with others it is helpful to draw the stretch and relevance matrix on a flip chart. When you have completed the matrix, select those criteria that give the appropriate amount of stretch and provide maximum relevance.

| Success criteria | Stretch rating* | Relevance rating |
| --- | --- | --- |

*Note: Scores nearest to zero are most desirable.

## Identifying success measures

Anyone who doubts the importance of success measures simply has to attend a slimmers' club for an evening session. Consider these comments from the manager of one of the most successful slimming clubs in England:

> Often the people who come to me have given up hope. They are maybe 50 pounds overweight, dislike themselves and have failed to lose weight many times before. The first thing that we do is give them an overall target weight and a weekly target. There is a formal weigh-in each week and all those who are on target get a magnificent round of applause. When someone reaches their target we have a ball! I give the men a present of a pair of boxer shorts in their new size and the women get a pair of knickers in black or red. Some are so excited that they frame their presents! Those who fail to achieve their weekly weight loss have a little bit of a hard time; they carry around a bag of potatoes to the weight that they should have lost. It's carrot and stick really.

This was a brilliant description of a truly motivating management technique that works reliably in some of the most intractable and difficult situations imaginable. Notice the emphasis on success criteria ('it is part of the contract that everyone who joins the club loses one and a half pounds each week'), on success measurement (the weekly weigh-in), and on appropriate celebration (the red knickers). This manager had enrolled her club members in feeling that the celebrations were important and that the symbolism meant something real. She pointed out that 'as well as losing weight, club members develop as people. They become more confident and feel their own power'. Achievement is essential for the development of human potential.

Although it may be unfashionable to admit it, success measures make it possible to exercise discipline and punish unacceptable behaviours. The managers of the most successful slimming clubs in England are given the opportunity to attend international conferences but need to be at their target weight. I was given this fascinating insight about one trip: 'As winners we all arrived at Heathrow excited, but had to be weighed-in. One girl was three pounds above her target weight. She was sent home. Of course, she was terribly distressed. But the point had to be made.' Failure to achieve success criteria has to be measured, registered and acted upon.

## TOOLBOX: ESTABLISHING SUCCESS MEASURES

Take each of the criteria that you have selected from the stretch and relevance matrix and enter them on the chart below. Then complete the other columns as suggested. If you are working with others, it is helpful to draw the chart on a flip chart. The chosen success measures should be written down.

| *Success criteria* | *How to measure* | *How often to measure* | *Who should measure* |
|---|---|---|---|
| | | | |

Carefully setting success criteria and establishing measures for success helps bring quality to the TOSIDPAR approach. Without this vital step too much is left to whim and fancy. A manager who does not have the criteria in place to monitor performance is like a craftsman who tries to construct a building without a tape measure.

A note of caution needs to be sounded. It may not be possible to go into full detail about success criteria and measures at this stage of the TOSPIDAR cycle. Only at the planning stage will all the necessary actions become apparent. However, experience teaches us that all possible success criteria and measures should be introduced at the earliest possible stage, as clarity about the definition of success shapes the next steps in the structured approach.

## SUCCESS MEASURES SKILLS AUDIT

Establishing success measures requires distinct skills. These are explored above, but it is important to relate the skills to yourself. Answer the following questions to audit your own skills.

1   Do you ask the question, 'what would be a successful outcome' several times a day?


2   Do you have measurable success criteria for each of your job objectives? What are they?


3   Do you have measurable success criteria for each of your career objectives? What are they?


4   Do you break tasks down into bite-sized chunks and set milestones for each? Give examples.


5   How often do you review both your successes and failures? What happens to the results of the review?


6   Do you celebrate success? Are the celebrations directly tied to the achievement of success criteria?


7   When you have to undertake a task that is difficult to measure, do you always seek to find some objective criterion with which to measure progress?

## YOUR PROJECT

In the previous chapter you established the objectives for the issue that you are using throughout this book. Set your success criteria and measures by answering the questions below:

1   What are your success criteria and success measures? Complete the table below.

| Objectives | Success Criteria | Success Measures |
| --- | --- | --- |
| | | |

2   How will you set milestones so that you know whether you are on track?

3   How do you know whether your capabilities will be fully stretched?

4   How will you reward success and learn from failure?

# 7 Step four Information collection

This step of the TOSIDPAR structured approach collects and structures *new* information that is necessary to enrich our understanding of what can be done. In the previous steps we used existing knowledge. This is often inadequate and we need to collect new relevant facts, opinions, feelings, ideas, and attitudes.

Information is drawn from many sources: experience, knowledge, external sources, and research. A blend of free-flowing creativity and highly disciplined analysis is required. The skills involved include creative thinking, identifying relevant data, collecting valid data, structuring data to make sense, identifying and meeting gaps in information. The information collection step is complete when options for action are identified and clearly laid out.

Let us assume that you are a member of the top management team of a company that produces a great variety of hose pipes.[1] You decide to expand the business by 5 per cent each year and improve profitability (which is poor at present) to above industry norms. All the necessary measures are in place to monitor your progress. What is the next step? You will need to collect and structure a large amount of data. For example, you need to know which of your lines is profitable and why. This must not be a superficial understanding. You will have to study the costs incurred with different batch sizes of hose, the costs of stock, the costs of meeting orders, and so on. You will also need to study the market and how it is changing; again your analysis cannot be done on the back of a cigarette packet – you will need to know, country by country, the changing market demand for different types of hose. But this is not all. You will need to gather data on the competition to understand the forces that affect industry profitability. You will need to study each of your competitors to determine their strategies, strengths, and weaknesses. Only when all this analytical work is done should you begin to think about what to do differently. You must avoid taking poor decisions based on an inadequate understanding of the situation: the information collection step is crucial.

The information collection step only works effectively when there is authentic interpersonal openness. One manager explained this point clearly from his own experience when he said:

> The previous managing director was a tyrant. Before one of his visits to our site we would be briefed not to say anything contentious. When he arrived we would all gather in the main office and he would say, 'Tell me your problems. I want to see all the cards on the table.' But nothing of any significance would be said.

We can conclude that no valid information flow could take place in this climate of interpersonal suspicion.

## HOW TO COLLECT INFORMATION

The information collection step has five stages. These are:

| | | |
|---|---|---|
| 1 | Identification of what information is needed | Answers the question: what do we need to know? |
| 2 | Establishing procedures to collect the missing information | Answers the question: how can we gather needed information? |
| 3 | Generating information through creativity and experiment | Creates and gathers information |
| 4 | Structuring information so that its meaning becomes apparent | Answers the question: how to structure the information? |
| 5 | Developing options for decision | Answers the question: what could we do? |

## Identification of what information is needed

Identifying what information is needed is one of the few tasks in the TOSIDPAR approach that often requires specialist expertise. For example, you may be asked to discover why radio transmissions from nuclear submarines are failing under certain meteorological conditions. This task needs to be given to experts in the arcane discipline of submarine radio communications; no matter how keen they are, a group of managers from a feather-plucking factory could not begin to cope. Feather-pluckers do not know what questions to ask in order to solve problems of military communication.

## TOOLBOX: IDENTIFYING INFORMATION REQUIREMENTS

The Post-it note technique is again useful here, especially if a proficient team can be gathered. Each team member writes on a Post-it note one category of needed information. Completed Post-it notes are arranged on a suitable flat surface and categorized. Once all of the information requirements are identified, for each piece of needed information it is necessary to ask: how can this information be obtained? Then a table is completed (perhaps on a flip chart) as shown in the format below:

Information requirements analysis

| *Information needed* | *How to obtain* |
| --- | --- |
| | |

## Establishing procedures to collect the missing information

This stage is particularly important for mystery solving. Remember that we have defined a mystery as an 'unexplained deviation from what is expected'. For example, if a computer system has been

satisfactorily controlling all stocks in a factory, but for some unknown reason now fails to do so on apparently random occasions,
this is a mystery. Two techniques are relevant: the first helps us
explore possible causes and the second enables us to plan information collection.

## TOOLBOX: EXPLORING POSSIBLE CAUSES

Information required for solving mysteries includes the
following:

- How can we precisely define the mystery?
- Exactly when did the mystery first occur?
- Do we have any ideas as to what changed to cause the
  mystery?
- What assumptions are we making about the causes of
  this mystery?
- When could this mystery have occurred, but didn't?
- How serious is the mystery?
- How urgent is the mystery?

## TOOLBOX: PLANNING INFORMATION COLLECTION

What? Who? When? How will the process be managed?
These are the key questions. An information collection plan
should be prepared (perhaps on a flip chart) as shown in the
table below:

Information collection plan

| *What?* | *Who?* | *When?* | *How managed?* |
| --- | --- | --- | --- |
| | | | |

## Generating information through creativity and experiment

Generating information through creativity and experiment is an activity that many people find difficult. At this stage of TOSIDPAR there is a great need to stimulate creativity. People are innately creative but are often blocked from using this capacity. Creativity is found in all areas of life. The marketing manager who finds new ways to approach a customer and the nursing home staff who find new ways to keep patients comfortable are as creative as the research scientist.

Creativity is heightened in four interlinked ways:

- *increased self-awareness* (fewer personal blocks to thinking creatively)
- *a range of creativity techniques* (procedures to structure the innovation process)
- *using the creative resources of others* (the innovative power of a team)
- *creating a creative climate* (supporting innovation by encouraging risk taking)

One day Albert Einstein was daydreaming in the countryside on a sunny day. He imagined that he went on a ride around the universe on a sun beam. His path through space followed a curved path, and through this fantasy he realized that space was curved, although it took him many years to prove it mathematically. Creativity, more than most other human attributes, has an element of magic. Yet it can be encouraged by understanding that the creative process has three stages: preparation, generation, and clarification.

### Preparation

For many people in a western culture, preparation requires quieting the left side of the brain (the part that deals with analysis, thought and logic) and allowing participation from the usually somnolent right side of the brain (the part that is artistic and intuitive). Freedom from demands and time to dream are required. Albert Einstein understood this when he once said that it was better for a thinker to be employed washing dishes than as a clerk since clerical work would occupy the mind and prevent new thoughts from occurring.

## Generation

Generation of ideas can be structured and you will find a number of suggestions on the next page. The key to idea generation is freedom from ridicule and permission to ignore the weight of tradition. A climate has to be created in which it is acceptable to think the unthinkable. This sounds grand, but it is not. A group of nurses in a casualty ward can generate many good ideas about improving their unit if they are given the opportunity.

## Clarification

Clarification of ideas is an essential stage. Creativity is untidy. Duplicate ideas have to be rationalized, and suggestions that offend values or objectives must be removed. As we will discuss later in this chapter, ideas have to be grouped into categories and elaborated before they can be evaluated.

Elias Howe was the first to develop a workable sewing machine.[2] His story makes the point that creativity and the unconscious mind are close companions. Howe had worked for years to perfect the machine but the shape of the needle eluded him. One night he had a dream that a group of savages had captured him and he had been commanded to finish the machine or be put to death. Howe was terrified but noticed that the savages were holding spears with eye-shaped holes near the points. He awoke with the inspired thought to shape a needle with a hole in the same position as the savages' spears. It worked; the last detail was perfected.

The most common creativity tool for generating ideas (which is almost never used correctly) is brainstorming. Brainstorming is essentially simple. It has been shown that the flow of ideas is curtailed whenever the process of evaluation begins. For example:

*Manager B*:  I want us to have a brainstorming session to develop some ideas for new products over the next five years.

*Manager A*:  I think that, with the latest developments in semiconductor technology, it should be possible to manufacture a low-cost robot for sheering sheep.

*Manager B*:  Never; there are too many variations in sheep for this to be a reality. It's a pipe dream.

*Manager A*:  I thought that it could be an idea we could follow up.

*Manager B*:  No, it's foolish. Who else has any ideas?

Such a process is a travesty of the brainstorming technique. Manager B should have said,

> I want us to have a brainstorming session to develop some ideas for new products over the next five years. We will take ten minutes initially. All ideas, no matter how wild, will be recorded on flip charts. No one is permitted to evaluate anyone's ideas until later. Let's go!

There are many other creativity techniques. Some favourites are outlined in the toolbox below.

## TOOLBOX: CREATIVITY TECHNIQUES

---

1  *Group brainstorming*: use the free association of a group to generate ideas.
2  *Meditation*: allowing your relaxed mind to flow around a topic.
3  *Metaphors*: look for similar situations in other walks of life which could provide an oblique insight into your situation.
4  *Silent brainstorming*: individuals privately brainstorm an issue, write down their thoughts, and share these with others.
5  *Wish lists*: ask what would we really like to happen (ignore today's constraints).

---

Very often managers are tempted to stop the creative process when they come to the first answer to a problem. However, this reaction prevents seeking other possible solutions. The tendency to be satisfied with the first answer is a profound creative weakness. Often, a deeper study reveals quite unexpected nuances and options. We have to learn to live with the void of uncertainty.

Whatever creativity techniques are used, there comes a time when they are inadequate: experiments are necessary. For example, I often use a construction task when conducting training programmes on effective problem solving. A team is asked to build a tower to support a heavy weight using only cards and paper. They usually brainstorm different ways to complete the project and uncover two or three methods that may be feasible. Then the team must experiment, as there is no way that brainstorming can give them the experience that they need to develop a winning design.

## TOOLBOX: CREATIVITY AND EXPERIMENT ANALYSIS

Generating information through creativity and experiment best progresses by asking the three questions shown in the table below:

### Creativity and experiment matrix

| What ideas are needed? | How can these ideas be sought? | What experiments are needed? |
| --- | --- | --- |
|  |  |  |

Experiment can be vital, and much thought should be invested in setting up effective experiments. Consider the example of Linn Products which make superb hi-fi equipment in a small factory in Eaglesham, Scotland.[3] Their managing director, Ivor Tiefenbrun, said, 'When we started in business [in 1973] ... we thought we were General Motors and had an assembly line. But we were always having to say "sorry" to our customers.' Often products were delivered more than nine months after the order was received and there were forty-seven costly buffer stores feeding the line. The assembly line, after the best managerial efforts in work study, took 27 minutes to manufacture one product. Then Tiefenbrun took the initiative: 'One day we asked one of the women on the line to collect all the parts she needed to assemble a turntable and to bring it back when she had got it together. She came back 18 minutes later.' Within months the assembly line was abandoned, buffer stocks were eliminated, and goods were being made on the same day that the orders were received.

Linn Products had tried many of the usual management techniques to collect information about their production problems but they had ignored the real source of insight – the women who actually assembled the precision hi-fi record turntables. By structured experiments the company made a breakthrough, and are now admired for their manufacturing brilliance.

As part of the experimenting stage it is important to ask the question: who has the information that we need? Often, managers ignore external sources of information that could provide a new perspective. Someone somewhere has almost always solved the same problem with which you are wrestling. Try to find such people and learn from them.

Creative information collection is particularly important for the management of opportunism. Of course, opportunities exist all the time but we often fail to recognize them. The following technique is relevant:

## TOOLBOX: IDENTIFYING OPPORTUNITIES

Answer the following questions:
- How are we identifying opportunities at the moment?
- What opportunities might occur?
- What exactly might these new opportunities be?
- How significant might these opportunities be?
- How urgent is it to take immediate advantage of these opportunities?
- Why have we not recognized these opportunities before?

The question of how much it will cost to obtain the wanted information is important because sometimes the likely benefit outweighs the cost. If you run a music company in Africa you may realize that you lack an appreciation of the current musical tastes of rural Zulu tribesmen in the age range of 35–50 years. However, the expense of collecting this information is unlikely to justify the costs incurred since this category of consumer buys few records. An assessment of cost benefit is always worth while.

There is another important concept which scientists and engineers regularly use but which has application to many managers. The concept is called 'confidence level'. Information is more or less certain. We know that the sun will rise tomorrow with a 99.9999$r$ certainty. But what toys will children want to buy next Christmas? The best guess of the marketing department may only have a 50 per cent confidence level ascribed to it. Whenever information is less than certain, give it a confidence rating.

## Structuring information so that its meaning becomes apparent

Structuring information so that its meaning becomes apparent requires a set of skills that all managers should possess.

The fishbone technique, which I learnt from Simon Majaro[4], has proved very useful for structuring information when we have a mystery or a difficulty with multiple causes. The technique is best illustrated in three diagrams. The example is a real-life mystery for John Coe, the manager of a large and busy restaurant. Sometimes diners complain that their meals arrive cold at the table. Why does this happen? Using the fishbone technique, the first step is to place the presenting mystery at the head of the fish.

**Fishbone diagram – the problem and its spine**

Food 'cold' at table

Then John and his team started the process of asking the question 'why?'. Each time a cause was found, it was entered as a bone of the fish.

**Fishbone method – problems and likely causes**

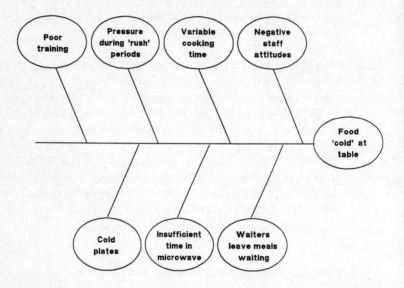

This provided more insight into the multiple causes of the mystery but the analysis was still too thin. John and his team began the process once again to find the second-level causes. Again the question 'why?' is asked, but this time for each bone on the fish. The second-level causes are entered as branches off each bone. The completed diagram is shown opposite.

Using the fishbone technique provided real insight into the causes of the cold food mystery. Finding a solution would mean addressing each of the first- and second-level causes. Until every one of the causes is understood and it is learned which causes are interdependent, it is impossible to take a good decision about what to do differently.

**Completed fishbone diagram**

Food 'cold' at table

- Negative staff attitudes
  - Low rewards for 'good' behaviour
  - Difficult to recruit staff
- Poor training
  - Managers not given training schedules
  - No designated trainer
- Pressure during 'rush' periods
  - Fixed staffing levels
  - No efforts to even out demand
- Variable cooking times
  - Chefs produce batches
- No effective call system
  - Walters cover excessive numbers of tables
  - Walters leave meals waiting
- Poor training for chefs
  - Lack of kitchen discipline
  - Insufficient time in microwave
- No effective plate warming system
  - Some cold plates

## TOOLBOX: STRUCTURING INFORMATION

Structuring information requires answering the three questions shown on the table below. The analysis should be
completed (perhaps on a flip chart) as suggested.

Structuring information plan

| What information needs structure? | What methods should be used? | Who should manage the task? |
| --- | --- | --- |
| | | |

## Developing options for decision

Developing options for decision is the final stage in the information collection step. Here we are concerned with elaborating all
of the feasible options to the point that they can be judged. Notice
that we separate elaborating options from making a judgement.
This is a crucial distinction and an example makes the point.

Sally Jones is a 45-year-old woman and the director of finance
for a local government administration. She has been divorced, her
children are virtually fully grown and she has set herself the objective of reviewing her career. She is reasonably wealthy and has no
dependants. One Sunday afternoon she begins to collect information that will help her make a decision. She asks: 'What do I
like doing?' The answers include: photography (she was an avid
amateur portrait photographer), teaching (she spent a few enjoy-
able months teaching 10- and 11-year-old children before deciding
to be an accountant), and studying yoga (which has been a continuing passion). Sally needs to explore each of the options further.
Relevant questions include: how much training is involved? Is
there an age barrier? What are the employment opportunities?
Until the options have been fully elaborated, Sally must hold
herself back from taking a decision.

## TOOLBOX: OPTIONS DEVELOPMENT PLANNING

A practical technique for ensuring that options are fully elaborated is shown in the format below. The table should be completed (perhaps on a flip chart) as shown:

Options development plan

| *What are all the feasible options?* | *What needs to be done to elaborate each option?* |
|---|---|
| | |

The information collection stage is especially problematic when the difficulties involved are emotional rather than objective. Assume that you are a manager and have James, a 62-year-old senior clerk, working in your team. Unfortunately, James's contribution has been declining as the date of his retirement approaches. You ask him why he has allowed his performance to deteriorate. He replies, 'I feel that I've done my bit. It's downhill from here. Why should I put in more? I won't get anything out of striving at my age.' As the manager you have a difficulty: you depend on James, but he is not pulling his weight and is a bad example to the others in the team. What do you do? The answer is, of course, that you follow the TOSIDPAR approach. But you will need to adapt the process as suggested in the example below.

First, you identify what information you will require. This will include finding out about James's motivation, determining the company's personnel policy in such matters, and discovering whether your colleagues have experience of successfully overcoming similar difficulties.

Second, you plan how to collect the information that you want to have available but do not have at the moment. This may be done by interviews, reading, discussions with experts, and so on.

Third, either alone or in an ad hoc team you use creativity techniques. Brainstorming all of the possible options – from promotion to enforced immediate retirement – provides a comprehensive list of possibilities. It may also be possible to experiment, for example by seeing how James responds to suggestions.

Fourth, information is organized so that its meaning becomes apparent. All of the various pieces of data must be laid out so that the whole situation can be clearly understood.

Finally, you lay out all of the feasible options for decision and ensure that they have been well thought through. This means that the costs, benefits, implications, and disadvantages are all articulated.

There has never been a time in human history when so much information is available. Computerized systems handle more magnitudes of data than the human brain. The manager's task is to use this wealth of information to improve effectiveness and not to become inundated. All too often we simply skim the surface of the meaning of information. Information collection skills developed for this step have wide application for all managers and professional workers.

It is important that all managers review their thought processes with the aim of developing ways of thinking that discern patterns in information. Managers need to be able to conceptualize, organize, categorize, and interpret events.

## INFORMATION COLLECTION SKILLS AUDIT

Information collection requires distinct skills. These are explored above, but it is important to relate the skills to yourself. Answer the following questions to audit your own skills.

1   Are you effective at identifying what information is needed? Give examples of times that you have done this.

2  How effectively do you plan to collect information in a systematic way? Give examples.

3  Do you have a set of creativity techniques in your toolbox? What are they?

4  Are you skilled at sorting out irrelevant information? Give examples of times that you have done this.

5  Are you skilled at categorizing information in terms of criticality, importance, and urgency? Give examples.

6  Are you skilled in finding techniques for collecting and analysing information? Do you have a toolbox of available techniques? What are the most commonly used tools in your toolbox?

7  Do you elaborate options for decision-making with total objectivity? Give examples of times that you have done this.

## YOUR PROJECT

It is time to continue work on your project. Answer the questions below:

1   What information is needed for you to make progress? Use the format suggested below.

| *Information needed* | *How to obtain* |
| --- | --- |
|  |  |
|  |  |

2   What procedures will you use to collect the missing information? Use the format suggested below.

| *What?* | *Who?* | *When?* | *How managed?* |
| --- | --- | --- | --- |
|  |  |  |  |

3   How can you generate information through creativity and experiment? Some of the following may be helpful: group brainstorming, meditation, metaphors, silent brainstorming, or wish lists (see page 70). Use the format suggested below.

| *What ideas are needed?* | *How can these ideas be sought?* | *What experiments are needed?* |
| --- | --- | --- |
|  |  |  |

4   Do you have a mystery or difficulty with multiple causes? If so, use the fishbone technique as suggested.

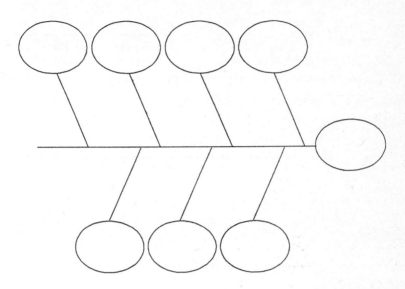

5   How can you structure the information that you now have available so that its meaning becomes apparent? Use the format suggested below.

| *What information needs structure?* | *What methods should be used?* | *Who should manage the task?* |
| --- | --- | --- |

6    What needs to be done to develop a clear statement of all of the feasible options for decision? Use the format suggested below.

| What are all the feasible options? | What needs to be done to elaborate each option? |
| --- | --- |
| | |

# 8 Step five
# Decision making

Step four of TOSIDPAR concluded by identifying all the feasible options for action, having elaborated each one. Logically, the next step is to choose one of the options: we need to make a decision. The decision-making stage is complete when a clear and wise choice has been made, and then communicated to all concerned.

Decision making is never easy because it involves weighing unlike attributes and assessing uncertainties. As a lover of horse racing, my father enjoyed gambling. He would spend many hours sitting at the kitchen table pondering encyclopedia-like volumes that contained up-to-date information on the form of each race horse. Having collected and assessed the available information he would eventually decide which horses to back, telephone the book-maker, and wait for the races to be run. Sometimes my father would make a good decision, sometimes not. But what interested me was that no matter how carefully he assessed the form of the horses, many unknown factors could intervene. For example, my father's chosen horse could lose because it fell in love with an attractive filly on the way to the racecourse or because it disliked the smell of the jockey's socks. Decisions are an attempt to predict the future and thus can never be taken without risk.

## HOW TO MAKE DECISIONS

Decision making has five stages:

| | |
|---|---|
| 1 Establishing an effective process for decision making | Answers the question: how should the decision be taken? |

| 2 | Clarification of the evaluation criteria | Answers the question: how should we evaluate the options? |
| 3 | Assessing the strengths and weaknesses of each option | Lists the merits of each option |
| 4 | Matching options and criteria | Answers the question: what is the best option? |
| 5 | Making the decision | Answers the question: what will we do? |

## Establishing an effective process for decision making

Imagine this situation: you are the President of the United States and you have been to a reunion party with some old army friends. Over drinks you swapped stories of those days long ago. You returned, somewhat the worse for wear, to the White House in the late evening. The First Lady, your wife, is not impressed with your blurred speech or your risqué stories of how you, and the boys, smuggled young ladies into your barracks on hot July evenings. You have a nightcap or two to help you cool down, start to think about the good old days, and eventually begin to walk unsteadily towards your bed, thinking of your first meeting tomorrow when you will be discussing controls on pesticides in the South American rainforests. Suddenly the red telephone rings: it's your chief of staff, who says, 'We have clear intelligence that an eastern bloc country is about to attack one of our allies with a pre-emptive strike. We have seven minutes to make a decision about whether to use our military forces stationed in the area. What shall we do, Mr President?'

This story demonstrates that the process for decision-making is as good as its weakest link. Even a well-designed process can lose its effectiveness from time to time. For speed and clarity some key decisions in the US political system are made by the President alone. But what happens if he is having an off day?

Decision-making processes have two dimensions: who is involved in taking the decision, and how the activity is managed.

In principle, the more people who are involved in a decision-making process, the less likely it is that the weaknesses or prejudices of one person can prevail. This is the principle on which the British House of Commons operates. It sounds to an outsider like playtime at a noisy infants' school, but the workings of the

Commons are designed to encourage argument and criticism. Twice each week the Prime Minister attends the Commons to answer any criticism of the government of the day. No quarter is given, and any weakness is seized upon with alacrity, like starving wolves attacking a piece of meat. Truth emerges through conflict.

Group decisions have another advantage: they give wider ownership of the outcome and bind the involved parties together. But including more people in the decision-making process adds complexity, takes time, and increases the risk of concluding with a fudged compromise that pleases no one.

The matter is important: it has been argued that the consensus-seeking approach to management decision making practised by most Japanese corporations is one of their recipes for national success. Japanese managers argue that the western decision-making style is macho, individualistic, and self-seeking. They believe it destroys the concept that a company is like a family in which all the members have something important to contribute.

In a hierarchical situation the boss can take an authoritarian decision or, at the other end of the continuum, can delegate to others. It is necessary to ensure that the 'ground rules' are explicit. In fact, there are eight decision-making options as shown below.

## Continuum of management decision making

- Manager decides and tells
- Manager asks, decides, and tells
- Manager proposes, listens, and tells
- Manager listens, proposes, tells, and listens
- Manager asks, listens, finds consensus, and announces
- Manager seeks consensus and goes with the group
- Manager delegates but requires to be kept informed
- Manager delegates fully

Prudent managers explain the appropriate ground rules for each new issue as it comes along. This greatly helps the teams during the decision-making process. Unfortunately, all too often the process is poorly managed. Meetings are handled badly, with the chairperson failing to steer the group through a structured approach like the one described in this book. Important items are dealt with at a gallop. It is vital that such malfunctions in the decision-making process are identified and remedied.

Poor meetings can be improved. When John Harvey-Jones

became chief executive of ICI, one of Europe's largest companies, he insisted that board meetings had to be conducted with adequate structure and strong discipline. No one was allowed to pass on a subject and all members were expected to give their views openly, cogently, and succinctly. The ICI board learned to work together efficiently and effectively.

Another potential hazard in the decision-making process is the risk of 'groupthink', a psychological phenomenon in which members of a close group all think alike. This important menace to the quality of the decision-making process was identified by a political scientist, Professor Irving Janus, who studied great political and military blunders to ask why those involved did not see obvious flaws in their arguments.[1] The answer is that members of groups look to other members for confirmation that their viewpoint is correct. But as groups become closer, something interesting happens: dissonant thinkers are expelled, contradictory opinions are derided, and individual perspectives become increasingly alike. 'Reality' is defined by what the other group members think, rather than by what the facts indicate. In such situations it is easy to see how the decision-making capability suffers.

## TOOLBOX: DECISION-MAKING PROCESS PLANNING

This tool will help you plan the appropriate process for making decisions. Three questions need to be answered, as shown in the table below.

### Decision making: process plan

| Who should be involved? | How should the decision be made? | How to avoid groupthink? |
| --- | --- | --- |
| | | |

## Clarification of the evaluation criteria

Clarification of the criteria that will be used to evaluate each of the options is, perhaps, the most important activity in decision making. Essentially, the idea is simple: in order to make a choice among options we need to establish the criteria that will be used for assessment. Articulating criteria clarifies choice. Managers often have difficulty in seeing how this principle is used. For purposes of explanation, 1 will describe a whimsical exercise undertaken by a group of (male) managers who were attending a course in the gambling and nightlife centre of Macao on the coast of the South China Sea. The managers were asked to determine the criteria they would use to select an activity for a good night in Macao. In addition, the managers were asked to specify whether each criterion was essential or desirable. An essential criterion was such that any option that did not have this attribute would be automatically excluded. A desirable attribute was one that gave advantage but was not decisive. Some desirable attributes are more enticing than others, and these were rated on a 1–10 scale.

**Criteria weighting**

*A night out in Macao*

| Criteria | Essential? | Desirable? |
|---|---|---|
| Low cost | | 3/10 |
| All can participate | Yes | |
| Able to work next day | Yes | |
| Be back in hotel by 11:00 p.m. | | 6/10 |
| All want to participate | Yes | |
| Nothing that we would not tell our wives about | Yes | |

Defining and weighting criteria may seem like an unnecessary and burdensome waste of time but, in reality, the opposite is the case. The rigour and discipline given by this technique adds greatly to the quality of the decision-making process.

## TOOLBOX: WEIGHTING CRITERIA

This tool will help you establish objective criteria with which to evaluate your options. First, free your mind of consideration of the options and answer the questions below in relation to a specific task or project.

- What are the essential criteria that our choice must meet?
- What are the desirable criteria that our choice should meet?
- How important are each of the desirable criteria? Give a score from 1 to 10 for each item.

**Criteria weighting**

*Objective*

| *Criteria* | *Essential?* | *Desirable?* |
| --- | --- | --- |

## Assessing the strengths and weaknesses of each option

Thus far we have a number of options (identified at the end of step four – information collection) but we have not attempted to assess the strengths and weaknesses of each option. For example, it may be that I have to go into town today and could make the trip by car, rail, cycle, pogo stick, or rickshaw. Each option has different strengths and weaknesses.

The assessment of strengths and weaknesses becomes more

important as the consequence of failure increases. A dull night out in Macau for a group of managers on a training course has little significance, but a nuclear reactor with a basic design flaw could result in a global crisis. Accordingly, the degree of care given to options analysis should vary according to the possible costs of failure.

The options analysis technique in the toolbox below provides a systematic and straightforward technique for assessing the merits of optional solutions.

## TOOLBOX: OPTIONS ANALYSIS

An options analysis should be prepared (perhaps on a flip chart) for each feasible option. Strengths and weaknesses are listed and given a weighting on a 1–10 scale. This is done using the format shown below.

**Options analysis**

*Option:*

*Strengths*                          *Weaknesses*

## Matching options and criteria

This step follows on logically. We have the options (developed at the end of step four – information collection) and we have the essential and desirable criteria to assess each option. All that remains is to put both together. This is best done on a matrix. Consider the example of the night out in Macao again. The managers had previously developed a list of options using a brain-storming technique that included:

1  A visit to the Lisboa nightclub to play roulette
2  A visit to the Oriental Delights Massage Parlour
3  Dining at Henrys, a typical Portuguese restaurant
4  A tour of the city by cycle-rickshaw
5  A swim in the pool at the Hyatt Hotel

When these options are placed on a matrix we see the following display.

**A decision matrix**

| Options | Criteria (see below) | | | | | |
|---|---|---|---|---|---|---|
| | 1 | 2 | 3 | 4 | 5 | 6 |
| 1 Visit to Lisboa nightclub | No | Yes | ? | No | Yes | No |
| 2 Visit to massage parlour | Yes | Yes | Yes | Yes | No | No |
| 3 Dinner at Henrys | Yes | Yes | Yes | Yes | Yes | Yes |
| 4 City tour | Yes | Yes | Yes | Yes | Yes | Yes |
| 5 Swim at Hyatt Hotel | Yes | Yes | Yes | Yes | No | Yes |

Just to remind you, the criteria were:

1  Low cost (desirable)
2  All can participate (essential)
3  Able to work next day (essential)
4  Be back in hotel by 11:00 p.m. (desirable)
5  All want to participate (essential)
6  Nothing that we would not tell our wives about (essential)

All the options except two (dinner at Henrys and the city tour) were excluded on the grounds that they failed to meet at least one of the essential criteria. The group decided to have dinner at Henrys and then take a tour of the city by cycle-rickshaw.

The matrix technique does not make the decision for you. If it were that simple, a computer could do it. But a decision matrix greatly increases objectivity. The technique is a useful tool for facilitating group approaches to decision making.

## Making the decision

This is the final stage. By now all the thinking should have been done. But there is a need to stand back and reflect before making a commitment. This helps to ensure that every possible avenue has been explored.

## TOOLBOX: DECISION MAKING

Take the options that are still viable and ask each of the ten questions below. Some questions will be relevant in each case.

1 How much will the decision cost?
2 What are the probable negative consequences of taking this decision?
3 What are all the things that could go wrong if we take this decision?
4 Who can prevent us from putting this decision into effect?
5 What are we losing by not taking one of the other options?
6 What strategic advantages (e.g. providing an improved competitive advantage) does this decision offer?
7 What values or beliefs underlie this decision?
8 How will people inside the organization interpret this decision?
9 How will people outside the organization interpret this decision?
10 What course of action do people feel a real commitment to see through? Where does the passion lie?

## DECISION-MAKING SKILLS AUDIT

Decision-making requires distinct skills. These are explored above, but it is important to relate the skills to yourself. Answer the following questions to audit your own skills.

1    Do you take great care to get the 'correct' people involved in decision-making? Give examples of times that you have done this.

2    Are you skilled in managing decision-making processes? What principles do you adopt?

3    Do you ensure that the ground rules for decision-making are always explicit?

4    Are you aware of the symptoms of 'groupthink'? Do you take all possible steps to mitigate the possible effects?

5    Do you systematically clarify the evaluation criteria you use to assess decision options? Are these criteria written down? Do you distinguish between essential and desirable criteria?

6    Do you explore all possible options thoroughly? Are your decisions rationally defensible?

7   Are you skilled at communicating your decisions to others? Do you always check to ensure that your statements have been correctly interpreted?

## YOUR PROJECT

Take the options that you generated in the previous step and answer the questions below:

1   How can you best identify and eliminate your personal bias?

2   How important is it to take the correct decision? Place a mark on the scale as appropriate.

| | | | | |
|---|---|---|---|---|

Highly significant

Slightly significant

3   What process will you use for decision making? Use the format suggested below:

| *Who should involved?* | *What process is needed?* | *How to avoid groupthink?* |
|---|---|---|

4    What criteria will you use to evaluate each of the options? Are they essential or desirable? Use the format suggested below:

| Criteria | Essential? | Desirable? |
| --- | --- | --- |
| | | |

5    Prepare an .analysis chart for all feasible options using the format below:

*Option:*

| Strengths | Weaknesses |
| --- | --- |
| | |

6    Develop a matrix matching options and criteria, using the format suggested below. (Adapt the chart as necessary to suit the number of options and criteria.)

| Options | Criteria (see question 4) | | | | | |
| --- | --- | --- | --- | --- | --- | --- |
| | 1 | 2 | 3 | 4 | 5 | 6 |

7    Make your decision, enter it in the space provided and answer
     the ten questions below:
     The decision is:

a    How much will the decision cost?
b    What are the probable negative consequences of taking
     this decision?
c    What are all the things that could go wrong if we take this
     decision?
d    Who can prevent us from putting this decision into effect?
e    What are we losing by not taking one of the other options?
f    What strategic advantages (e.g. providing an improved
     competitive advantage) does this decision offer?
g    What values or beliefs underlie this decision?
h    How will people inside the organization interpret this deci-
     sion?
i    How will people outside the organization interpret this
     decision?
j    How should we communicate our decision to others?

# 9  *Step six*
# *Planning*

The purpose of the planning step is to provide a detailed programme to effect your decisions. This requires new skills and procedures. We are primarily concerned with gathering and organizing resources to get things done. The planning stage is complete when we have a detailed plan and thought-through methods of dealing with potential snags.

The quality of an organization is greatly influenced by the quality of planning. Consider the Disney theme parks. Every aspect of the operation is planned with meticulous precision. The guide on the jungle boat ride works to an eight-page script with another three pages of permitted variations. Rubbish bins are moved nearer to or farther away from the ice cream stands according to weather predictions. A vastly complicated computer system controls all the attractions.

Despite the vital importance of planning we must not allow ourselves to imagine that everything can be planned in advance. Life is not like that. Charles Handy tells a superb story which makes the point.[1] He was given a career briefing by his new employer thirty years ago and shown a map of his future progress, culminating in his becoming the chief executive of a subsidiary in a foreign country. Now the job does not exist; neither does the company or the country. Plans are only valid for a limited period of time.

# HOW TO PLAN

Planning has four stages:

| | | |
|---|---|---|
| 1 | Specifying what has to be done | Answers the question: what needs to be done? |
| 2 | Identifying what might inhibit or stop you | Answers the question: what could get in the way? |
| 3 | Organizing | Answers the question: how should resources be managed? |
| 4 | Managing change | Answers the question: how can leadership be given? |

## Specifying what has to be done

This step can require a great deal of detailed thought. Imagine that you are asked to mount a multinational research expedition to the South Pole. Everything from thermal socks to an amateur's dentistry kit has to be provided. Each item needs to be chosen, ordered, checked, listed, and packed. It is a huge task whose success depends on planning with painstaking detail.

Such planning tasks are everyday occurrences. More than 22,000 separate items have to be loaded onto a jumbo jet before it flies. The police in a large city have to schedule a thousand officers to manage the morning rush hour traffic. We live in an age of complex planning.

It was a remarkable man, Ralph Coverdale, who introduced me to the expression: 'What has to be done?' Coverdale realized that many projects fail, not because the people involved lack capability, but because people fail to use their existing wisdom, skills, and experience. He pointed out that many managers do not ask the right questions at the right time. The 'what has to be done?' question provides the perfect stimulus needed to change gear from the heady excitement of the previous step – decision making – and begin the painstaking planning process.

At its simplest level the 'what has to be done' stage requires merely a list of tasks. This afternoon we are going on a picnic. What has to be done? Well, the food has to be purchased, sandwiches have to be made, children's games dug out of the loft, umbrella repaired, wine put into the refrigerator, and so on. A list of tasks is adequate to manage the preparations for a picnic.

## TOOLBOX: SIMPLE PLANNING

> One technique which has proved most useful is the Post-it note method that we have used before. Each member of the planning team separately writes down all of the tasks that have to be done, ensuring that only one task is written on each piece of paper. The task notes are positioned on a suitable flat surface, moved into logical clusters, and recorded as a plan.

When a task becomes more complex, a more elaborate planning process is needed. Say you decide to travel by train from Toronto to Rio de Janeiro. Some of the tasks that you have to complete, like obtaining a visa, take longer than others. You cannot start one task, say, obtaining a Brazilian visa, until your passport has been returned from the Panama visa office. Accordingly, you must schedule the tasks in a logical order. Another complication is that not all the tasks are as important as others. It is not a disaster if you forget your electric nostril hair trimmer, but it is if you fail to get a visa to enter Brazil! Tasks therefore vary in terms of their importance or criticality.

Scheduling and criticality of tasks is important whenever a complex project is planned. Computer programmes that perform critical path analysis or similar techniques are available to run on anything from a lap-top to a mainframe. But the subject is too large to deal with here and you are advised to seek further guidance if your work involves planning major projects.[2]

All planning tasks are based on certain assumptions. For example, Chairman Mao, as China's ruler, decided that sparrows were taking too much of the crop, thereby denying food to the masses. It was decided that war would be declared on the humble sparrow. Up and down the land villagers were mobilized to capture sparrows and bang gongs to prevent the birds from landing. A crescendo of sounds filled the air. It worked! The sparrow population plummeted, but then insects, now relieved of their predators, began to proliferate. This demonstrates that an effectively executed plan can result in disaster if the earlier stages of TOSIDPAR have been inadequately considered.

## Identifying what might inhibit or stop you

This is an interesting and vital stage. Many managers have a clear notion of what they want to do but are flummoxed when asked how they could achieve their objectives. There are many barriers: the task seems too daunting, they lack the skills, resources are lacking, and so on. In such a situation there is one technique that helps us sort out all the different elements: force field analysis.

Like all good models, force field analysis is basically simple. The idea is this: all situations can be described *at a moment of time* as being in equilibrium. There are forces promoting change – the driving force – and forces which are preventing the change from happening – the resisting forces. Equilibrium is the point at which the forces are in balance. An example explains the approach.

Let us say that Harry, an overweight man, decides to slim. It is not the first time that he has set himself this objective and, this time, he decides to investigate why he remains corpulent. The driving forces promoting change are: vanity, the advice of his doctor, and the fact that his clothes no longer fit. The resisting forces are: Harry's love of beer, his refusal to count calories, and lack of weight reduction targets. For the time being, the forces for change are counterbalanced by the resisting forces and the resulting equilibrium is a persistently paunchy Harry. In order to understand the force field analysis technique, we display the forces on a diagram; the vertical line represents equilibrium, which is positioned at Harry's present weight of 200 pounds. His aim, of course, is to move the equilibrium line to the right.

**Force field analysis diagram**

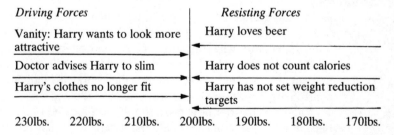

| *Driving Forces* | *Resisting Forces* |
|---|---|
| Vanity: Harry wants to look more attractive | Harry loves beer |
| Doctor advises Harry to slim | Harry does not count calories |
| Harry's clothes no longer fit | Harry has not set weight reduction targets |

230lbs.    220lbs.    210lbs.    200lbs.    190lbs.    180lbs.    170lbs.

The main advantage of the force field analysis technique is that it assists us in planning change. In Harry's situation, there are only three things he can do; first, he can strengthen the existing driving forces; second, he can add new driving forces; and third, he can weaken or eliminate the resisting forces.

Figure 11 is the simplest possible illustration. A full force field analysis will include a measured scale for the equilibrium line (to define success criteria) and arrows of an appropriate length to represent the relative importance of each force. It is not unusual for there to be 20 arrows on each side of the line, each representing a distinct force.

## TOOLBOX: FORCE FIELD ANALYSIS

Select a suitable topic and undertake a force field analysis by completing the steps below. It often helps to work with several other people using a flip chart.

- Draw the equilibrium line and put a scale on it.
- Brainstorm all the driving and resisting forces and position them on the chart. Be exhaustive. Try to assess the relative importance of each force and draw an arrow of appropriate length.
- Ask: 'What can we do to strengthen the existing driving forces?' Consider each force separately.
- Ask: 'What can we do to add new driving forces?'
- Ask: 'What can we do to weaken or eliminate the resisting forces?'

## Organizing

Organizing can be a huge topic: it all depends on the extent of the task. However, there are three principles that apply to all organizations, no matter what their size. These are best expressed as questions: First, on what principle should we allocate tasks to individuals? Second, how should the work of individuals be controlled? Last, how should work be co-ordinated?

When we consider how tasks should be allocated to individuals, one principle becomes evident: the extent to which jobs can be broken down into simple elements determines the approach. Some jobs – for example, working as a counter assistant in McDonald's – can be learnt in a matter of days. Other tasks, such as neurosurgery, take many years to learn. The longer it takes to learn a job, the more discretion can be given to the job holder.

The work of individuals can be controlled in three ways: by plan, by results, or by policies. Control by plan means that each individual plays a predetermined part in a master plan and the manager acts like the conductor of an orchestra. Control by results means that there is a predetermined set of targets (success criteria) but the individual makes his or her own plans to achieve the required results; here the manager sets objectives and monitors performance but avoids hands-on administration. Control by policy means that the individual knows the corporate's broad objectives and boundaries and then takes initiatives within these guidelines; in this situation the manager is a scene-setter, coach, and educator.

The co-ordination of work happens in four ways: informally, through a supervisor, by standardization, and as a result of psychological programming.

Very small groups can co-ordinate their work through informal agreement; no authority or systems are needed. But as the complexity of the task grows, so the need for communication increases and the informal method becomes unworkable. The solution is to appoint a supervisor who co-ordinates the activities of others and gives instructions.

However, even the most brilliant supervisor becomes overwhelmed when complex tasks have to be managed. The only way to co-ordinate activities is to develop systems that standardize behaviour. If you want to see an example of standardization in operation, just go down to your local McDonald's. One special form of standardization is psychological programming, in which the employees' attitudes and beliefs are shaped so that they almost cannot help but behave in approved ways.

Research in organization theory assists us to plan more effectively.[3] Briefly, the lessons are these:

- There is no best way to organize.
- However, some ways of organizing are better for you than others.

Two variables are important. The first is uncertainty, the extent to which you can define what you will be doing next year. The second is diversity, the extent to which your organization has to undertake a wide range of tasks.

Predictable situations can be planned in advance, and the organization fine-tuned to cope. As uncertainty and diversity increase, so the amount of information requiring to be processed also increases. New mechanisms for decision making are needed. At least one of these four strategies must be used:

■ Create 'slack' resources – have extra people/facilities to handle the unexpected.
■ Create self-contained tasks – organize around products, markets, and so on.
■ Invest in information management systems – use systems, computers, and so on to make information digestible.
■ Set up 'integrating mechanisms' – link people by communication, teamwork, and so on.

As complexity increases further, decision making must be moved down the organization. Those who know best (rather than those who have formal authority) must become decision makers; however, such arrangements prove difficult to control. A well-run organization capable of managing uncertainty is one that has found ways to integrate specialists without reducing their expertise.

The greater the degree of uncertainty, the harder it is to plan. New ways of thinking about organization are required. In a rapidly changing environment, instead of seeing an organization as a machine for implementing plans we must learn to see it as a dynamic bundle of related competencies and capabilities which can be put to use depending on the demands of the moment.

We can begin to put this theory into practice by completing an analysis of a given plan using the following format.

**Planning the organization**

| How should tasks be allocated? | How should tasks be controlled? | How should tasks be co-ordinated? |
| --- | --- | --- |
| | | |

## Managing change

Change always requires that people behave differently. This is never straightforward. Accordingly, the tactics of managing change need to be worked out well in advance. The most important issue is to identify who is going to be the change leader.

A change leader takes an embryonic idea and drives it through. Such people are passionate about their project but are willing to work within the organization. Often their political skills are highly developed. They continue despite setbacks and disappointments. Change leaders are willing to consider unorthodox views and will not allow themselves to be defeated by the bureaucracy of the organization.

The commitment of the change leader is vital. Texas Instruments conducted a survey and found that nearly all unsuccessful new product launches had a non-volunteer change leader. Change leaders need a 'sponsor' to give support, especially in the early days when their idea looks unworkable.

Peters and Waterman describe the role of the change leader vividly. He or she 'is not a blue-sky dreamer or an intellectual giant. The champion may even be an idea thief. But above all, he is the pragmatic one who grabs on to someone else's theoretical construct if necessary and bullheadedly pushes it into fruition.'[4] Peters and Waterman also point out that organizations fail to innovate when they have a 'misplaced belief in planning, a misunderstanding of the disorderly innovative process, a misguided trust in large scale, and an inability to comprehend the management of organized chaos'.

Edward Schon, of the Massachusetts Institute of Technology put the point superbly when he wrote:

The new idea either finds a champion or dies ... No ordinary involvement with a new idea provides the energy required to cope with the indifference and resistance that major technological change provokes ... Champions of new inventions display persistence and courage of heroic quality.

Change leaders practise 'chunking' and 'small wins'. Breaking large tasks into bite-sized chunks offers important advantages. People often fail because they try to achieve too much at once. They go for a big breakthrough and become demoralized when they don't achieve their aim. Better progress is made when the 'small wins' approach is used.

## TOOLBOX: SMALL WINS

---

The 'small wins' approach helps break down major changes into achievable elements. Follow these guidelines:

- Set goals that can be achieved by the end of next week.
- Reward and celebrate success.
- Encourage people (but be authentic).
- Keep the goal 'alive' by showing interest and commitment.
- Look backwards at achievements and allow confidence to grow.

The following format will help you to plan a process of small wins.

**Small wins worksheet**

---

*Project:*

---

*Change manager:*

---

| *Who?* | *What?* | *When?* | *Where?* |
| --- | --- | --- | --- |
| | | | |

---

## PLANNING SKILLS AUDIT

The skills of the effective planner are different from those needed for the other steps. Orderliness is essential. These are the key skills:

1   Are you skilled in organizing thoughts? Are you able to handle a great deal of complex information at one time? Give examples.

2   Can you identify a logical order for activities and put things to be done into a sequence? Give examples.

3   Do you describe events in orderly ways? Give examples.

4   Do you involve others in planning so as to get input from all those who may be affected? Give examples.

5   Do you prepare lists or charts to manage complex interrelationships? Give examples.

6   Do you establish effective procedures for controlling and co-ordinating people in organizations? Give examples.

7   Do you adopt an attitude of 'I'm going to get this done come hell or high water?' How strongly do you follow through? Do you allow events to demoralize you?

## YOUR PROJECT

In the previous step you decided what you would do. Take your analysis further by answering the questions below:

1   What has to be done? Use the Simple Planning Tool described on page 96.

2   Prepare a force field analysis diagram as suggested on page 97. Draw the equilibrium line and, if possible, put a scale on it. Brainstorm all the driving and resisting forces and position them on the chart. Be exhaustive. Try to assess the relative importance of each force and draw an arrow of appropriate length. Extend the diagram below as much as necessary.

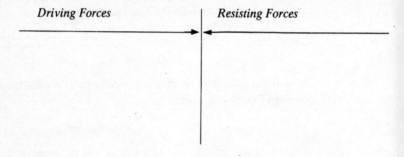

*Driving Forces*  |  *Resisting Forces*

3   Answer the question: what can we do to strengthen the existing driving forces?

4   Answer the question: what can we do to add new driving forces?

5 Answer the question: what can we do to weaken or eliminate the resisting forces?

6 Complete the chart shown below.

| *How should tasks be allocated?* | *How should tasks be controlled?* | *How should tasks be co-ordinated?* |
| --- | --- | --- |
| | | |

7 Complete the 'small wins' worksheet shown below.

*Project*

*Change manager:*

| *Who?* | *What?* | *When?* | *Where?* |
| --- | --- | --- | --- |
| | | | |

8 How can you make the most efficient use of resources?

9  How can greatest priority be allocated to the most significant tasks?

10  What precisely can go wrong? Can you reduce the likelihood of potential problems or difficulties? Do you need contingency plans to minimize potential hazards? How will you know when to implement your contingency plans?

11  How can you make the plan visible and clear to all concerned?

12  What training in techniques (e.g. critical path analysis, networking, bar charts) are relevant for you?

# 10  *Step seven Action*

The action step is the culmination of the TOSIDPAR structured approach. There are many forms of action: a new machine is ordered, an army patrol mounted, a bridge built, a marketing plan launched, and so on. Action may be simple, like sending a telex, or complex, like constructing a wing for a new aircraft. The action stage is complete when a finite cycle of activities has been completed and it is possible to stop and review the effectiveness of what you have done.

Action needs to be undertaken with confidence, vigour, will-power, objectivity, skill, adaptability, precision, and teamwork.

*Confidence* comes from knowing what you have to do, and feeling able to do it. Participating in the first six steps of TOSIDPAR builds confidence. When this is done the manager knows that he or she has been through a careful, meticulous, logical, and creative process which provides the best possible foundation for action. Even though the activity may be novel, the TOSIDPAR methodology always proves to be a guide, mentor, and friend.

*Vigour* is a more personal attribute. It comes from being in contact with one's own life force and will-power. Life force is a relatively little understood concept. Briefly, the idea is this: we all have a source of life energy deep within us (you only have to see the passion of a baby crying with rage to see this) but the way in which we react to some experiences creates inner barriers that begin to cut us off from the life force. These inner barriers can become so impenetrable that we are unable to feel any surge of inner energy. Impediments to being in touch with one's life energy are difficult to remove, but sometimes this can be done through counselling, which enables the original feelings to be relived.

*Will-power* sounds like an old-fashioned notion: there are echoes of the Old Testament in the word. But the concept of will-power is due for a renaissance. It is a much-needed personal quality in today's world. Will-power means the ability to decide to do something and then follow through, despite all obstacles. It is the ability that gets fat people slim, climbers to the top of Mount Everest and businesses from being one-man bands to multinational corporations. Will-power is the capability to say 'I will' and mean it. Many people misunderstand the concept. They think of will-power as a given attribute, like being born with red hair. This is incorrect: will-power develops and should be encouraged. Fortunately, some of the developments in self-managed learning are making progress in this direction.

*Objectivity* is the ability to be passionately committed to a project whilst holding part of oneself in reserve: being objectively observant and dispassionately monitoring what is happening. For many people this is difficult. It requires that the manager never fully relaxes, even when things are going well. The questioning process is always continuing:

- Are we doing the right things?
- Could we do things better?
- Are our assumptions correct?
- What signs will tell us that things are going wrong?
- How can we deal with the unexpected?
- How effectively are activities being co-ordinated?
- At what stage do we need to look at our fundamental principles afresh?
- How can morale be kept up?
- How are standards to be maintained?

*Skill* is a prerequisite for the successful execution of many tasks. A balloonist who is not an engineer cannot build a successful bridge, no matter how much enthusiasm is dedicated to the task. Often it is necessary to develop skills prior to taking action. In general, training needs are poorly identified and change leaders should pay especial attention to this issue.

*Adaptability* can be defined as the ability to accommodate constructively to new situations. This is an important attribute in the action step because few things go as predicted. The effective manager recognizes when conditions render the current plan inappropriate. He or she rapidly recycles, using the gates concept (see Chapter 12) and re-entering TOSIDPAR at the appropriate step (see the figure overleaf).

*Precision* is necessary for effective action. A friend told me a story which makes the point. He was travelling in the United States and stayed at a hotel owned by a nationwide chain. All was well, except for the cockroaches in the bathroom. My friend decided to respond to the request for complaints letters which was in his bedroom and wrote to the president of the hotel chain. In time he received a reply which began: 'I was personally very distressed to hear of your problem with cockroaches in one of our hotels.' All would have been well had it not been for the Post-it note stuck to the letter which read, 'Send the son of a bitch the cockroach letter'.

*Teamwork* is essential for many action programmes. Rarely is an activity to be carried out by one person alone; often a team is required. All teams need to be well constructed, strongly motivated, and efficient. Teamwork is greatly assisted when the whole team uses the TOSIDPAR process. The approach becomes a common language, a standard methodology that binds members together. The structured approach described in this book is essentially participative because many of the techniques are designed for use by groups. But structure alone is insufficient to provide a positive climate. The team manager must engender, through his or her own behaviour, openness, confrontation, mutual support, and a high degree of commitment to team goals. Things must be done. In the action step it is imperative that the activities of different individuals and groups are co-ordinated towards the common goal. Systems need to be in place to maintain ongoing co-ordination and pick up information which is fed back into the system to trigger remedial action.

**Recycling in TOSIDPAR when action does not go as planned**

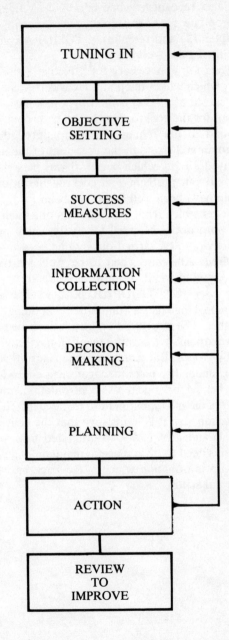

## ACTION SKILLS AUDIT

1   Do you have a great deal of self-confidence? Give examples.

2   Do you have a great deal of vigour? Give examples.

3   Do you have a great deal of will-power? Give examples.

4   Do you have relevant skills? Do you develop missing skills in a systematic way? Give examples.

5   Do you have a great deal of adaptability? Give examples.

6   Do you demonstrate a great deal of precision? Give examples.

7   Do you generate effective teamwork? Give examples.

## YOUR PROJECT

Answer the four questions below and then put your plan (as defined in the previous step) into effect!

1   What can you do to increase the confidence of yourself and any others involved?

2   What can you do to increase the vigour of yourself and the others involved?

3   What can you do to increase the skill of yourself and the others involved?

4   What can you do to increase the adaptability of yourself and the others involved?

5   Now: get into action!

# 11 *Step eight*
# *Review to improve*

You might have thought that action was the last step. This is a natural conclusion but a shortsighted one. We need to learn from every experience in life and use the insights gained to improve in the future. Effectiveness is learnt in the real world, not in the class-room. What happens, for good or ill, is our teacher, coach, and mentor.

All too often we dash from one thing to the next without taking time to review. In fact, this final step – review to improve – is the most neglected of all. Managers usually say that they believe in the merits of review but, in practice, they do not find the time to do it.

You notice that the step is called 'review to improve'. The last two words are important. The purpose of reviewing is to enhance individual competence and develop organizational capability.

## HOW TO REVIEW TO IMPROVE

The review to improve step has four stages.

| | | |
|---|---|---|
| 1 | Review performance against success criteria | Answers the question: how successful were we? |
| 2 | Review individual effectiveness and develop an improvement plan | Answers the question: how could I improve? |
| 3 | Review organizational effectiveness and develop an improvement plan | Answers the question: how could we improve? |
| 4 | Celebrating success | Answers the question: what is the appropriate reward? |

## Review performance against success criteria

A review of performance judged against success criteria looks at whether you achieved all that you set out to do. In step three – success measures – you established criteria and measures for each of your specific objectives. Well, now the chickens have come home to roost: you have to see whether you have performed as expected, differently than expected, or better than expected.

Why does this matter? Results are the test of the efficiency of your process. If you have failed, and the causes are obscure, then you have a mystery. Everything we have said about mystery solving applies to you. Effective managers are those who can reliably deliver results.

Performance review requires that you answer these questions:

- Have you achieved all your objectives?
- If you have fallen short, what are the reasons?
- Are these reasons genuinely beyond your control?
- Did you achieve your success criteria?
- If not, why not?
- In retrospect, were your success criteria adequate (stretching, relevant, and achievable)?
- Did you use the minimum necessary resources to achieve your results?
- Have any other individuals or groups tackled the same job and done better?
- If so, what is your explanation for falling short?

## Review individual effectiveness and develop an improvement plan

The individual learning review and development of an improvement plan provides an opportunity for each person involved in the project to obtain some personal learning. The most effective learning review methods require participants to assess their own and the others' capabilities. This gives positive motivational advantages, as people are much more likely to act on the basis of their own conclusions. But self-review is never sufficient. Unless feedback is received, people find it difficult to rate themselves objectively. People tend to ascribe their failings to external rather than internal factors.

Such feedback can be extremely significant. However, as with many powerful tools, it can be abused. Everyone, including the change leader, should be both a giver and a receiver of feedback. All those involved need to find ways of giving feedback that result in each participant stronger and more effective.

The guidelines below suggest how feedback can be given in constructive ways. The skills of giving feedback become an extremely valuable management asset; additionally, they improve many aspects of one's personal life.

- Give feedback on specific behaviours (rather than general comments about performance) and ask the person to state how he or she judges the results.
- Suggests that the participants compare different aspects of their performances relative to one another (rather than with other people).
- Involve the participants in detailed identification of their own weaknesses/strengths (rather than superficial and glib statements).
- Move towards a concrete action plan for building on strengths and remedying weaknesses.
- Avoid using strongly authoritarian approaches which have been shown to be counter-productive. Avoid any hint of blame or retribution in your voice.
- Tell people you will be giving feedback and receiving feedback regularly (make it part of 'the culture').
- Give the feedback sessions sufficient time and undivided attention. Try to make them open-ended.
- Tell people exactly what they did well.
- Tell people what their performance means to you, the company, and the customer.
- Be truthful.
- Be careful about timing; do not wait too long before giving feedback.

Feedback is a gift. We often think that our experiences and opinions are likely to upset or damage if they are voiced. Very often the opposite is true. By withholding our reactions we deprive others of information which could be extremely helpful for them. Interestingly, when we have unexpressed negative thoughts, this is often observed by the other person as aloofness. Subtle non-verbal signals leak our real feelings.

One technique, called the 'I appreciate/I wish' process, introduced to me by Larry Porter, has proved very useful for facilitating interpersonal feedback in project groups and teams during the review to improve step, but this technique must only be used with volunteers.[1]

## TOOLBOX: I APPRECIATE/I WISH

Each team member writes a message to each of the others involved. He or she says what they appreciate about the other person's contribution and what they would like the other person to do differently. When all the messages have been prepared they are signed and passed to the addressees, who should receive one message from everyone else. Each person then has a turn in the hot seat, when he or she reads out all the messages and asks for clarification where necessary. Any decisions as to what to do differently are the responsibility of the individual. The feedback messages should be laid out as below:

I appreciate/I wish message form

| *Message to:* | *From:* |
|---|---|
| *I appreciate* | *I wish* |

## Review organizational effectiveness and develop an improvement plan

The organizational effectiveness review, and development of an improvement plan, has a similar function to the individual review, but this time the focus is on the organization. Everyone who can make a contribution is gathered together and asked to consider the effectiveness of systems and organization using the following questions:

- What were the strengths in what we did?
- What, if any, skills or competencies did we lack?
- How satisfied are we with the quality of organization?
- What areas could be improved in leadership?
- What areas could be improved in systems?
- What areas could be improved in communication?
- In what aspects of the TOSIDPAR approach are we strongest?
- In what areas of the TOSIDPAR approach are we weakest?
- What processes or activities would have helped to achieve a better quality result?
- Did we spend more money or resources than necessary? If so, what lessons can be learnt for the future?
- If we were to tackle the same job again, how would we approach it differently next time?

It is important that review to improve takes place in relation to both successes and failures. One manager described his organization as being motivated by a fear of failure and commented, 'we dwell on things that go wrong, we call them post-mortems, but never discuss things that go right'. Unless success is analysed with the same vigour as error the review to improve step fails to energize and nourish people.

The purpose of review to improve is to interfere with the typical cycle of action–reaction–action. We deliberately introduce this step to enforce a 'stop'. The purpose is to prevent meaningless repetition of ingrained habits. A deliberate and rigorous review provokes a critical reappraisal which increases the chances of improved quality and effectiveness in the future.

## Celebrating success

This is an important postscript to this step. Anthropologists studying tribal societies report that rituals for celebrating success are universal: as if something deep in mankind seeks recognition through an expression of joy, letting go, and mutual admiration. Celebration is a source of nourishment for the human spirit. If a project is terminated without marking the importance of the effort expended then much of the significance is lost. There can be no rules for managing celebrations. One group may enjoy a boozy weekend sailing, another a night at the opera, whilst a third may simply enjoy having a few beers together. But celebrate you must.

Truly experiencing failure is the other side of the coin. If a project goes wrong, and the blame belongs to those involved, then the failure must be admitted. Recriminations are often counter-productive but analysis is essential. Often the deepest learning comes through the consideration of failure. Then the energy of disappointment needs to be transformed into resolve to do better next time.

## REVIEW TO IMPROVE SKILLS AUDIT

1    Do you make time to review to improve? When was the last time that you did this? How often do you review to improve?

2    Do you make sure that reviews to improve are positive occasions? How do you ensure that no one is humiliated in the process?

3    Do you analyse the reasons for both successes and failures? Give examples of when you have done this.

4   When a project is complete do you systematically identify what you have personally learnt from the experience? Give examples.

5   When a project is complete do you ensure that all those involved systematically identify what they have learnt from the experience? Give examples.

6   Are you skilled in giving feedback to others in ways that help them to learn? Give examples.

7   Do you ensure that successful projects conclude with a celebration? How effective are you at managing celebrations? Give examples.

## YOUR PROJECT

You have almost completed your project. It is time to step back and review how well you have done. Answer the questions below.

1   Review your performance against your objectives and success criteria (see your answers to steps two and three) by answering the questions below.

■   What have been your successes?
■   Have you achieved all your objectives?
■   If you have fallen short, what are the reasons?
■   Are these reasons genuinely beyond your control?

- Did you achieve your success criteria?
- If not, why not?
- In retrospect were your success criteria adequate (stretching, relevant, and achievable)?
- Did you use the minimum necessary resources to achieve your results?
- Have any other individuals or groups tackled the same job and done better?
- If so, what is your explanation for falling short?

2   Review your personal performance and develop an improvement plan by undertaking the analysis below.

---

*Following my review of performance, in future I will . . .*

---

| *Do more of* | *Do less of* | *Start to do* | *Continue to do* |
| --- | --- | --- | --- |

---

3   If your project involved others, get together with those involved and review your effectiveness and devise an improvement plan by answering the questions below.

- What were the strengths in what we did?
- What, if any, skills or competencies did we lack?
- How satisfied are we with the quality of organization?
- What areas could be improved in leadership?
- What areas could be improved in systems?
- What areas could be improved in communication?
- In what aspects of the TOSIDPAR approach are we strongest?
- In what areas of the TOSIDPAR approach are we weakest?

- What processes or activities would have helped to achieve a better quality result?
- Did we spend more money or resources than necessary? If so, what lessons can be learnt for the future?
- If we were to tackle the same job again, how would we approach it differently next time?

4  Have you effectively celebrated success? If not how will you do this?

# 12 *Using TOSIDPAR in practice*

You have now studied and practised the eight steps in the TOSIDPAR structured approach. Are you apprehensive? Most people feel that if they used the full TOSIDPAR approach the result would be snail-paced problem solving and paralysed analysis. Don't worry! There are shortcuts, but try not to use these as an excuse. There will be times when you need to use most of the steps, stages, and tools in TOSIDPAR. But often you will not need to go through a full eight-step circle. It is better to choose the most appropriate step and focus on that, rather than trying to skim the surface of the whole approach.

This shortcut technique is called 'gatekeeping'. The essential step, relevant to every mystery, assignment, difficulty, opportunity, puzzle, or dilemma is tuning in. At the end of the tuning in step you ask, 'Through which gate to I wish to go?' The following questions will help you:

- Do you need to become clearer about what you want to achieve? Then you need to enter step two – objective setting.
- Do you need to identify clearly how you are going to judge your performance? Then you need to enter step three – success measures.
- Do you need to collect information so as to evaluate different approaches to the problem/decision? Then you need to enter step four – information collection.
- Do you need to choose between possible alternative courses of action? Then you need to enter step five – decision making.
- Do you need to turn a choice about what to do into a definite action plan? Then you need to enter step six – planning.

■ Do you have all the necessary plans to proceed? Then you need to enter step seven – action.

■ Have you completed activities and reached the end of a cycle? Then you need to enter step eight – review to improve.

Gatekeeping identifies particular techniques and concepts relevant to your needs at the time. These are most helpful when dealing with real work situations. Practice the use of gatekeeping and you will be surprised at its practical value.

You now have a bag of problem-solving tools and you need to use each of the tools on real challenges. In the introduction to this book we covered the basic groundwork. Now that you have come to the end of your journey it is useful to review the key points.

Remember, TOSIDPAR is not easy to master. This integrated toolkit needs to be followed as a strict discipline until you find that the TODISPAR approach has become second nature. Then you will be able to use it with poise and flexibility. Initially you may be confused and overwhelmed. Hang in there! With practice it will become second nature, and the disciplines will be embedded in your unconscious repertoire of skills.

As we said in the introduction, the TOSIDPAR structured approach is the hallmark of a professional who favours thoroughness rather than cosmetically attractive quick solutions. It is vital for all managers to be able to use the full TOSIDPAR approach. TOSIDPAR is a rigorous discipline dedicated to providing truly effective action programmes that get things done.

This book will be beneficial to you only if you use the TOSIDPAR approach on real issues. Look for opportunities. Work problems are ideal, but there are many domestic situations which offer the chance to practise. Perhaps you are about to buy a new car or go on holiday: try to TOSIDPAR it!

Don't forget: it is not going to be easy to become more effective in the art and science of getting things done. You are not starting from scratch. Over the years you have met many mysteries, assignments, difficulties, opportunities, puzzles, and dilemmas – and done your best. Some of your habits will be unconstructive or inefficient. These negative habits need to be detected, understood, and changed.

The craft of structured problem solving must be learnt in the real world. No matter how much theory you acquire, the only valid tests are those that life throws at you. So, practise the stances and skills explained in this book as much as you can. Stand back, review your successes and failures, and challenge yourself. Then celebrate your growing competence.

To conclude this book, list opportunities over the next month for using the TOSIDPAR approach. Remember the ancient recipe for craftsmanship: 'practice, practice, practice!'

# Notes

## 1 INTRODUCING TOSIDPAR

1 See Henry Mintzberg, *The Nature of Managerial Work* (Englewood Cliffs, NJ: Prentice-Hall, 1973).
2 There are several other structured approaches, the best known of which are the Coverdale method and Kepner Tregoe. See Max Taylor, *Coverdale on Management* (London: Heinemann, 1979) and Charles H. Kepner and Benjamin B. Tregoe, *The Rational Manager* (Boston, Mass.: Kepner Tregoe Inc., 1986).

## 3 WHEN IS A PROBLEM NOT A PROBLEM?

1 Michael Porter, *Global Competitive Advantage*, in press.
2 Dr R. Baker, *The Mysteries of Migration* (London: Macdonald Futura, 1980).

## 4 STEP ONE: TUNING IN

1 Sun Tzu, *The Art of War* (London: Hodder and Stoughton, 1981).
2 This framework is drawn from Kenneth Blanchard, Patricia Zigarmi and Drea Zigarmi, *Leadership and the One Minute Manager* (London: Collins, 1986).
3 Dealing with emotional blockages is beyond the scope of this book. Much useful insight can be gained from *Games People Play* by Eric Berne (Harmondsworth: Penguin Books, 1977).

## 5 STEP TWO: OBJECTIVE SETTING

1  The insightful term 'compelling vision' was coined by Warren Bennis in *Leaders,* by W. Bennis and B. Nanus (New York: Harper & Row, 1985).
2  For a further discussion of the importance of values in management see Mike Woodcock and Dave Francis, *Clarifying Organizational Values* (Aldershot, England: Gower, 1989).

## 7 STEP FOUR: INFORMATION COLLECTION

1  The author is indebted to Marcus Alexander for providing this example.
2  Adapted from a story in *The Intuitive Edge: Understanding and Developing Intuition* by Philip Goldberg (Los Angeles: Tarcher, 1983).
3  *Business World, Sunday Times,* 29 October 1989, p. 48.
4  Simon Majoro, *The Creative Gap* (London: Longman, 1988).

## 8 STEP FIVE: DECISION MAKING

1  See Irving Janus, *Victims of Groupthink* (Boston, Mass.: Houghton Mifflin, 1972).

## 9 STEP SIX: PLANNING

1  Charles Handy, *The Age of Unreason,* (London: Business Books, 1989).
2  D. Lock, *Project Management* (Aldershot: Gower, 1989).
3  For further insight into the topic of organizational design, see Jay Galbraith, *Designing Complex Organizations* (Reading, Mass.: Addison Wesley, 1973).
4  From *In Search of Excellence* by T.J. Peters and R.H. Waterman (London: Collins, 1982).

## 11 STEP EIGHT: REVIEW TO IMPROVE

1  Included in *50 Activities for Unblocking Organizational Communication* by Dave Francis (Aldershot: Gower, 1987).